EMPIRE made

THE HANDY PARKA POCKET GUIDE TO ALL THINGS MOD!

BY TERRY RAWLINGS AND KEITH BADMAN

DEDICATED TO THE MEMORY OF RONNIE LANE

First published in 1997 by:
Complete Music Publications Ltd,
Bishop's Park House,
25-29 Fulham High St,
London SW6 3JH.

℗ & © Complete Music Publications Ltd 1997.

A Writing Wrongs book.

Written and compiled by
Terry Rawlings & Keith Badman.

Designed by
Mark Waine and Terry Rawlings
at Red Snapper Design.

Jacket designed by
Terry Rawlings and Paul McEvoy at MC80.

A CIP catalogue is available from the
British Library.

ISBN: 0951720686

Printed and bound in the UK by Bath Press.

It was 1962, and I was heading up the Uxbridge Road for the 10,000th time, on my Vespa 125, which incidentally cost me exactly 'one two five' quid, which always struck me as funny. I was making my way to the 'Barbasque Club' which was a little underground drinking club opposite Ealing Broadway tube station. Now by Underground I don't mean it was an illicit, 'word of mouth' in the know only type of cool hip club. It was that it was held underground in the basement. Little Jazz bands would play there in the evenings, and it was popular with what was the tail-end of the 'Beatnik' scene, and the early mods. The club's owner -----, re-christened it on these nights 'The Moist Hoist' on the account of there being no ventilation, and the condensation would literally run down the walls, so much so that they had to erect a tarpaulin canopy over the stage to stop the bands from getting soaked from the dripping ceilings. Rhythmn & Blues was still in its infancy in England around 1962, I was singing with Alexis Korner's 'Blues Incorporated', who were really the pioneers of R & B in the UK. We had been playing the Marquee regularly and had been doing great business around London, building a solid following of Blues fans. We were getting so popular, that Alexis had this idea of us having a club of our own, A 'Blues' club. This was what lead me back to the 'Moist Hoist' to see the owner, in order to point out to him that R & B was the 'in-thing' and that the Alexis Korner band was what the club needed. The club was agreeable, and I told Alexis and his partner Cyril Davies about my find. I Arranged to take the pair back to Ealing, in order to check it out. I picked them up in Wardour Street a few days later on a Aerial Hunt Master 650 twin- with a double adult side car, If I was to be precise, wasn't very mod! The three of us, Alexis and Cyril in the side-car, headed West up the Uxbridge Road once again. It's a frightening thought------------, that it could of all ended just there. But thankfully we arrived safely. Alexis and Cyril loved the place, and renamed it 'The Very Imaginative Ealing Club'. The rest is history, 'Mod History' if you like. It became the most popular club in London, and established both Alexis and Cyril as the founders and forerunners of 'British R & B'.

Alas, all good things come to an end, when Alexis and Cyril went their separate ways, and split the band.Charlie Watts, the drummer, joined the interval band The Rolling Stones, and I formed the Art Wood Combo, later shortened to the Artwoods. By 1964, the movement had become so big and we all had become so well known,that forming new bands was inevitable, and we were all assured an audience. We had no worries for our futures. I had formed the Artwoods by pinching Jon Lord, our Hammond player, Derek Griffiths our guitarist, and Don Wilson our Bass player, from a band called Red Bloods Blusicians and a local drummer I had known from West Drayton called Reg Dunnage. Don Wilson was unfortunately injured in a van crash and decided to leave and was replaced by Malcolm Pool, who had been with The Roadrunners. Reg Dunnage replaced himself with a job at London Airport, so we got Keith Hartley to complete the picture.

We were all typical little Mods. We all bought scooters,except for Derek who was Posh! He bought an MG. I had a Lambretta 150, which I bought from Stirling Scooters in West Drayton. We had suits made, Hush-Puppies, the whole bit. We were playing The Twisted-Wheel and The Mojo Club in Manchester, Eel-Pie Island in Richmond and the 'l00 Club' in Oxford Street , London, all big Mod clubs. We hit it just right, live wise. My two youngest brothers were also in bands. Ted, who didn't follow the mod trend, joined Colin Kingwells Jazz Bandits. But little Ronnie formed The Birds, who for my money, were THE top Mod Band, they really looked the part, because they were much younger, and they were the centre of the West Draytron scene if you like, although there was only one other band in it, they were Cliff Bennett & The Rebel Rousers, whose bass -player was Frank Allen, later to join The Seachers. We would all rehearse in the West Drayton Community Centre, which was transformed every Friday night into 'The Birds Nest', in honour of The Birds weekly residency.

London had all these little scenes going, us lot in the west, The Who in Shepherds Bush, and later the Small Faces in the East, all with their own little Mod following, it was an incredible time. We would meet The Who in a little all-night cafe, again down the bleedin' Uxbridge Road, and check each other out, with the shoes and clothes etc.

Looking through this little book it struck me just how many of those bands and the players in them went on to achieve so much, and how many of their audience or fans if you like, stayed with them, and evolved with them, through the 60's, 70's and 80's, and in a lot of cases into the 90's. All I can say is that they must have been pretty good to start with.

It's true what they say about Mods, you can still spot the originals today, although they are a bit older, and of course there are new generations that come along every few years, it's a real English phenomenon, and it's lovely to see a humourous book like this devoted to it!

CONTENTS

THE ACTION

The Who and The Small Faces are the two bands that readily spring to mind when recalling the mid sixties Mod scene. However, The Action, an unjustly overlooked five piece group from Kentish Town arguably epitomised the excitement of the London club scene. Starting life in 1963 as The Boys, a backing group for singer, Sandra Barry, (releasing a single on Decca and later a single under their own name on Pye) the group were spotted by Beatles recording producer George Martin and signed to Parlophone. They released five singles during their two year lifespan, between 1965 and 1967, including superlative covers of little known soul and Motown classics (including Chris

which saw the group's Mod threads evolving into Kaftans, they disbanded in 1967.

Classic Action line up:
Reggie King (vocals), Alan 'Bam' King (rhythm guitar), Mike Evans (bass), Roger Powell (drums), Pete Watson (lead guitar)
Recommended Listening:
"I'll Keep Holding On" PARLOPHONE R5410
"Shadows and Reflections" PARLOPHONE R5610

WE'LL GIVE YOU NO BULL!!
JUST YOU HEAR THE RECORD
by
THE ACTION
"LAND OF 1,000 DANCES"
b/w "IN MY LONELY ROOM"
on PARLOPHONE R5354
Recorded by: GEORGE MARTIN
Management: RIKKI FARR
Agent: COLIN HOGG, Harold Davison Agency Ltd., REG 7961

Kenner's "Land of a Thousand Dances", The Marvelettes "I'll Keep Holding On". and Martha and The Vandellas "In My Lonely Room"), as well as strong originals ("Never Ever", "Shadows and Reflections"). With the Beatles' producer (and the Fabs' seal of approval behind them) plus a strong Mod following up and down the country, the reasons for their failure to chart remain a mystery. After recording demos for an aborted album' "Brain" ,

ACTION!

TAKE	SCENE
THE FAN CLUB	SEE INSIDE

THE ACTION invite you to get out of your mind at the MARQUEE STUDIO thurs. FEB. 10th. 1 p.m. 90 wardour st.

THE ACTION!

MICK EVANS /BASS GUITAR, REGGIE KING /VOCALS ALAN KING /RHYTHM GUITAR /VOCALS PETE WATSON /12 STRING LEAD GUITAR ROGER POWELL /DRUMS

Marquee Artists Agency Ltd, 18 Carlisle Street, London, W1   Management : Rikki Farr Tel. GER 6601 2 3

ADAM ADAMANT LIVES!

(BBC1 1966-67)
Adam Llewellyn de Vere Adamant (played by Gerald Harper) is drugged and frozen alive in ice in 1902 by his arch-enemy "The Face" (see that's mod) played by Peter Ducrow. This is where he remained until he was discovered and thawed out, alive and intact, into the crazy world of 1966. Upon his re-generation in swinging London, he meets two companions, Georgina (played by Juliet Harmer) and valet Simms (played by Jack May), who accompany him through his modern day tackles with crime and villainy. When the series returned to BBC1 in December 1966, Adam's old adversary "The Face" joined him, where they regularly crossed swords. This is the synopsis for this BBC1 adventure series, comprising of 29 x 48 minute episodes, adequately described as a cross between Batman and The Avengers.

corporation had fulfilled their contractual obligations of two screenings of a particular episode, the video-tapes were sadly 'wiped' to be re-used for something else. For the trivia buffs amongst you, the most watched episode of "Adam Adamant Lives" was 'A Vintage Year For Scoundrels' on June 23rd 1966, when over 5.3 million people tuned into BBC1 to watch the latest adventure. Suave and sophisticated Gerald Haper in 1969 went on to portray the 'cool and calculated' character "Harper" for Yorkshire ITV.

Incidentally, the theme tune to the series was sung by Kathy Kirby. The series was one of the first to be recorded on 'video-tape', and this is one of the main reasons why only a handful of the shows still survive. Once the

ALFIE

(Film 1966)
Michael Caine's wonderful portrayal as the carefree, womanising cockney won him a new army of fans, and gave his acting career a much needed boost. The film, based on the play by Bill Naughton, concerns Alfie's moral dilemma as to whether bachelor life is "Bloody marvelous or not?". Among the woman he mixes his emotions with are Shelley Winters, Millicent Martin, Julie Foster, Shirley Anne Field, Vivien Merchant and Jane Asher. (114 minutes- colour. The title track for the film was sung by Cher, minus Sonny. However Cilla Black had an inferior top ten hit with the song in March of the same year.)

My name is Maurice Micklewhite...
nah, it hasn't the same ring to it

IRWIN ALLEN

Famous for his 1960's television 'cliffhanger' serials, where the heroes never came home, thus rendering his programmes 'never concluded'.

Born in New York City in 1916, the only son of Joseph and Eva Davis, Allen began adult life as a student at Columbia University, later moving on to radio station KLAC, in Hollywood, where he worked as a commentator. His first taste of the film business occurred when he found work as a film editor for 'Atlas Features Syndicate' (again in Hollywood). After taking further jobs up the ladder (which included work as a television producer) Allen, was credited as associated producer on the film 'Where Danger Lives'. Further film credits included 'A Girl In Every Port' (1952), and 'The Big Circus' (1959). But it was his television work in the 1960's that he will be best remembered. Beginning in 1963 with "Voyage To The Bottom Of The Sea" starring Richard Basehart and David Hedison, then quickly followed by "Lost In Space" in 1965, starring Guy Williams and June Lockhart. In 1966 Allen, took the adventure idea, literally into another dimension with the launch of "The Time Tunnel", where two scientists (Doug and Tony) are helplessly 'stuck in time'. Incidentally, this serial was the only one that Allen actually reached a conclusion with. The final part sees our heroes go through the 'Time Tunnel' and land up back on the Titanic (as they appeared on the very first episode). (How annoying was that.) Allen saw the conclusion that they "would never get out of the 'time tunnel' and forever be lost in time!". This, considering that the series was aimed for youngsters, was deemed unsuitable, and therefore the final episode now appears cut prior to their reappearance on the ship.

1969 saw "The Land Of The Giants", a special-effects extravaganza, with humans crash landing in their space ship on an alien planet and, (as the title suggests) facing the perils of giant people. But by the 1970's, Allen concentrated on less elaborate themes, with programmes such as 'The Swiss Family Robinson', 'The Return of Captain Nemo', 'Code Red' and 'Alice In Wonderland'. But with the constant re-runs of his 60's TV shows now playing to a new generation of fans across the world, the late 1980's saw Allen approach the original cast of "Lost In Space" for a 'spin-off' series called "Still Lost In Space", complete with a now 32 year-old Billy Mumy (Will Robinson) and Marta Kristen (star of the 1974 American soft-porn film 'Gemini Affair') who played Judy. But due to the death of the father, legendary American actor and TV star of "Zorro!" Guy Williams, the idea was naturally scrapped.

Allen was also producer for his biggest cinema hit, the memorable 1974 Warner Brothers/20th Century Fox disaster film "The Towering Inferno" starring, amongst others, Paul Newman and Steve McQueen, and producer/director on another disaster film, the 1979 "Beyond The Poseidon Adventure", starring Michael Caine, who also just happened to be in Allen's classic 1978 'multi-million dollar flop' "The Swarm". (A film he would rather forget!)

His offices remain to this day in Columbia Pictures, Burbank, California, USA

Classic Watching:
The Seaview Submarine, crashing on the same rock every week...unmissable

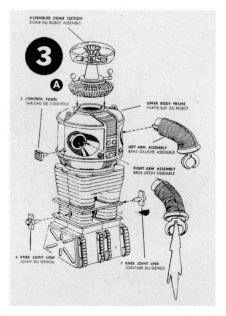

Gerry, along with his wife Sylvia will always be remembered for their ground-breaking work in 'television puppetry', which reached new heights with some of the most memorable children's action series ever seen on British television.
In fact he only went into the art of 'puppetry' when the production company he was in charge of, (AP Films of Maidenhead), was commissioned by Granada ITV in Manchester, (famous for the long-running 'soap opera' Coronation Street) to produce 39 x 15 minute episodes of a series called "Four Feather Falls", featuring a puppet character called Tex Tucker, a wandering cowboy with the voice of (from Norwich, it's the quiz of the week) Nicholas Parsons and singing talents of Michael Holliday (who was to die tragically in 1963). The success of the series, when first screened on ITV in 1960, prompted Anderson to work on another 'puppet' series.
The next series "Torchy", (1960/61) was commissioned by Associated/Rediffusion, where it ran for 52 x 15 minutes, and featured the stories of a toy child who ran away from a toy shop and became friends with a black cat called 'Footso'. Next was "Supercar" (1961/62, ATV, 39 x 25 minutes) the Sci-Fi adventures of a 'supercar' (Well!!!) that could speed

above the ground. The test-pilot and superhero, was Mike Mercury. Then followed "Fireball XL5" (1962/63, ATV/ITC, 39 x 25 minutes) featuring Venus, Steve Zodiak and Robert The Robot (whose voices were supplied for the first time in an Anderson series by Sylvia & Gerry Anderson respectively). "Stingray" (1964/65, ATV/ITC, 39 x 25 minutes) was centred around stories set in the year 2000 and featured the crew of the submarine 'Stingray', commanded by Captain Troy Tempest (with a characature resembling American actor James Garner) with assistance from his first mate Phones, and the underwater-breathing beauty Marina. The series also marked the first to be made in colour, purely for sales to the American television market.
1965 and 1966 saw production of his most famous and elaborate adventure series "Thunderbirds" (ATV/ITC, 32 x 48 minutes). The adventures of the family-based members of 'International Rescue', which included the permanently office bound father Jeff Tracy, and his five sons. Scott (who piloted 'Thunderbird 1'), Virgil ('Thunderbird 2'), Alan ('Thunderbird 3'), Gordon (co-pilot 'Thunderbird 2' and pilot of 'Thunderbird 4' for underwater work) and John who had the unenviable shift of being left on his own ('Thunderbird 5'). Ably assisted

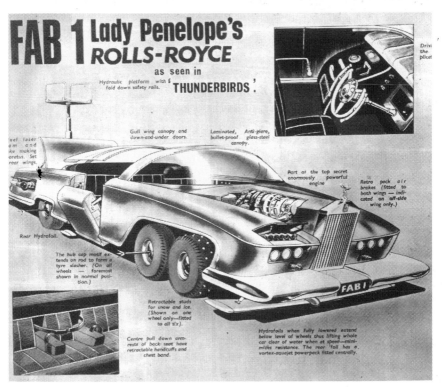

by Brains, and London Agent Lady Penelope (featuring the voice talents again of Sylvia Anderson) with her Chauffeur and former tea-leaf Parker. There were two 'Big-Screen' spin-offs. "Thunderbirds Are Go!" (1966) and "Thunderbird 6" (1968).

Gerry Anderson and his new production crew (named 'Century 21', which also spawned a weekly adventure comic) continued with production at Stirling Road on the Slough Trading Estate in Buckinghamshire, with "Captain Scarlet & The Mysterons" (1967/68, Century 21/ITC, 32 x 25 minutes), a 21st Century 'indistructable' space-warrior who was a cross between Elvis & George Best, (voiced by Francis Mathews) who is constantly faced by the threat of the Mysterons, led by Captain Black (a former colleague of 'Spectrum').

Joe 90 (1968/Century 21/ITC, 30 x 25 minutes) concerned the heroics of a 9 year-old boy whose 'superhero' characteristics' were sparked off by a special pair of glasses. He was assisted in his adventures by his step-father professor and his deputy.

In 1969, Gerry Anderson moved into the idea of combining live action and puppetry. His first attempt "Secret Service" (starring Stanley Unwin) was only received by certain ITV regions, while the impossibly Mod "UFO" was a great success. (1969/70, Century 21/ITC, 26 x 50 minutes), which meant moving his operations to studios at Pinewood Studios.

Starring Ed Bishop as a commander of the future (the 1980's). The organisation

MORE MONEY—MORE FUN—IF YOU DON'T SMOKE

10 cigarettes a day cost £30 a year or more
15 cigarettes a day cost £45 a year or more
20 cigarettes a day cost £60 a year or more

was called 'SHADO' (Secret Headquarters Alien Defence Organisation) and was situated below a film studio (actually Elstree, in Hertfordshire). George Sewell and the gorgeous Gabrielle Drake (phwooah), later of "Crossroads" fame, were the noted co-stars.

"Space 1999" (1975 - 1977, ITC, 48 x 50 minutes) was Anderson's last great success, featuring husband and wife team Martin Landau and Barbara Bain (who met on the set of the 1960's innovative American series "Mission: Impossible"). The series focused on a colony of earth people who became reluctant inter-stellar explorers.

Gerry also went on to produce the series "The Protectors" (1972-1974) starring 'The Man From Uncle's Robert Vaughan and Nyree-Dawn Porter, "Terrahawks" (1979) and in most recent years "Space Patrol", where he again returned to work at Pinewood Studios in Iver, Buckinghamshire.

Incidentally, in the mid. 1970's Gerry sold all-rights to his catalogue of programmes to ITC, hence the reason why no mention of his name appears in Modern day merchandising of "Thunderbirds", "Captain Scarlet" etc.

> **Anderson note:**
> *While Joe 90 sent out its well meaning message that weedy geeky nine year old goodie goodies could be cool wearing glasses, it inadvertently gave birth to the now common place school yard referral to any weedy, geeky nine year old goodie goodie as "Oi, Joe 90"*

THE ARTWOODS

The amalgamation of two West Drayton bands, The Artwood Combo and Red Blood's Blucicians in 1964 resulted in creating simply the Artwoods. Fronted by Art Wood himself (who along with Charlie Watts had been a founding member of Alexis Korner's Blues

Massacre and released an EP of the same name in a sad attempt to cash in on that year's gangster craze, but this too failed to chart and Art left the band. They left behind a brilliantly recorded catalogue and gave the world of progressive rock two of its more colourful characters in the shape of their Hammond player, Jon Lord, later of Deep

Incorporated in 1962). The band built up a solid reputation as the hardest working outfit on the R & B circuit. The band's live show and set of Chicago blues standards together with their own carefully crafted blues originals received the sort of recognition the band craved when blues godfather Little Walter said in November 64 after catching the bands show "Truthfully I thought that white boys couldn't play the blues but these boys were playing the hell out of the music. Them boys were as pure in the blues as many a negro group back home. There's many a player in the States who couldn't keep up with them." High praise indeed, but it wasn't enough, The Artwoods signed to Decca Records and released a string of brilliant singles including the near hit 'Sweet Mary', an EP 'Jazz in Jeans' and one album entitled 'Art Gallery'

Purple (and a inspiration for the legendary Spinal Tap spoof) and drummer Keef Hartley who played at Woodstock and for artistic reasoning known only to himself wouldn't allow his performance or name to be used in the film, soundtrack or video, thus insuring

which had a huge target logo on its cover. However, despite several successful tours of the UK, Europe and Poland (with Elkie Brookes) and a solid following, the band's records made little impact. Inevitably the band concluded that fame was to sadly elude them and changed their name in 1967 to the ill advised Saint Valentine's Day

he was never heard of again.

Classic line-up: *Art Wood, VOCALS, HARMONICA; Derek Griffiths, LEAD GUITAR; Malcolm Paul, BASS; Jon Lord, HAMMOND ORGAN; Keef Hartley, DRUMS.*
Recommended listening:
"I Take What I Want" DECCA F12384
"Sweet Mary" DECCA F12015
"Goodbye Sisters" DECCA F12206

The term Pop Art refers to a stylistic development in Western art which occurred roughly between 1956 and 1966 in Great Britain and the United States. That roughly translates to a whole bunch of artists led by Roy Lichtenstein, and Andy Warhol, in thriving on the rich pickings provided by Pop groups, Blake went on to design album covers for The Beatles (Sgt Peppers), while Warhol designed for the Velvit Underground. The Who conscious of never being true Mods embraced the Pop Art movement wholly and adapted a complete new look for the band that drew heavily on the comic book creations

America, and Peter Blake in England Painting and drawing soap packets, soup tins, coke bottles, and comic strips. These new artists were the first to combine Art and Pop music, at a time when the entertainment industry was of Lichtenstein and the military imagery of Blake. It gave rise to that ole Mod main stay the target image and for this alone we should be eternally grateful. Other Pop Art influenced groups were The Creation, The Smoke, and The Eyes.

Early Mod pop arty targety imagery

The Mojos take advantage of handily placed target on a wall at the Elephant & Castle's Butts House showing their Mod alliance. Eventual Spiders From Mars drummer and Bluesbreaker member Aynsley Dunbar (see Bowie), second from the left, and actor Lewis Collins, far left. Trivia note: The target still survives to this day.

JANE ASHER

Jane was born in London on April 5th 1946, She made her first professional appearance in 1951 in the film "Mandy", and then in 1960, made her West End stage debut in the play "Will You Walk A Little Faster".

It was on Thursday April 18th 1963 that, following her pose, screaming for The Beatles in the 'Radio Times' report on the Royal Albert Hall concert, that she first met the group, and subsequently began dating Paul McCartney. They were inseparable for years, and finally became engaged on Christmas Day 1967. She announced to millions of television viewers that their engagement was off during the peak-time BBC1 show "Dee Time" in June 1968. To this day, Jane still refuses to discuss her relationship with Paul. During the decade, she is also fondly

Decca Records in house photographer Dave Wedgebery take advantage of Decca's close proximity to the Elephant & Castle's Butt's House once again and drag new signings Unit four plus two around the South London shopping centre, just as the MoJos were leaving!

remembered for her portrayal of the teenage runaway in the 1966 Michael Caine film "Alfie".

Today, married to cartoonist Gerald Scarfe, she now makes ends meet by baking cakes on Pebble Mill and such like.

Above: a yoof-ful Janet Street Porter looks towards the future and avoids getting her round in.
Centre and below: Eerie picture premonitions as Weller moves away from Bruce and Rick on the sleeve of their 4th Polydor single while three chords, Buddy Ascott, Chris Pope and Martin Mason are pictured prior to sacking their singer (not pictured) Billy Hassett.

You'll get all the

TOP POPS

at **Boots** RECORD SHOPS

A WHOLE SCENE GOING

(BBC1)
Produced between January 5th and June 15th 1966.

In another version of what was to become known as 'youth TV', BBC1 patented this 'happening' weekly programme, successfully combining a blend of pop, youth culture and current affairs. Primarily aimed at the 'thinking teenager', this Wednesday night tea-time show was regularly hosted by Barry Fantoni (cartoonist for both the 'Observer' and 'Private Eye') and Wendy Varnals (whose only previous claim to fame was her cleverly scripted lines being edited out of the Beatles second movie "Help!" in 1965).

Other regular features included the 'Mary Quant' inspired opening titles, which included a guitar-playing Eric Clapton, an agony corner with 'Aunt Sally' (better known as Scotch-lass Lulu) and contemporary spokesmen, like comic-genius Spike Milligan, discussing issues raised by the young viewers.

During it's six month run, 'A Whole Scene Going' tackled a wide range of subjects, among them "The Roaring Twenties- Are They Coming Back?"(they didn't), "Cheap Travel In Scandinavia", "Jazz & Pop - Behind the 'Iron Curtain'", "Mary Quant and John Michael On Spring Fashions", "Bed-Sits In London" and "Modesty Blaise- Is She The Female Answer To James Bond?"

Naturally, the biggest attraction were the pop stars. Among those featured were Peter & Gordon and The Dave Clark 5 (March 9th), Herman's Hermits (March 23rd), Small Faces (April 6th) and The Kinks and The Yardbirds (June 8th). That particular show also included Ravi Shankar discussing 'Indian pop music'.

Another feature was location reports. Amongst the special reports singled out were Johnathan King and his proteges Hedgehoppers Anonymous (February 2nd), Eric Burdon and The Animals (February 23rd) and an 'on tour' report featuring Dave Dee, Dozy, Beaky, Mick & Tich clowning around, (pre-Monkees style) in Paris.

'A Whole Scene Going' was also noted for the chance it gave for the fans to ask questions directly to the stars themselves, in the "Hot Seat". These included Rolling Stone Mick Jagger, singers Dusty Springfield and Roy Orbison. From the world of acting came 'Harry Palmer' and 'Alfie' star, Michael Caine, while the world of sport was represented by Chelsea footballer Peter Osgood.

As the programme was transmitted live, it's not surprising to discover that only three shows still survive in the BBC archives.

These being the first ever broadcast from January 5th featuring The Who (on film and in the studio) including Pete Townshend's famous "Hot Seat" interview, where he described the 'stereo' on The Beatles albums as "flipping lousy!!", the show from January 26th featuring The Pretty Things, and the afore mentioned June 8th edition with the Kinks, Yardbirds and Shankar. (At least one other survives 'unofficially'. The edition from January 19th, where The Kinks made their first appearance on the show).

THE AVENGERS

The ABC Television series, "The Avengers", made it's debut on ITV during 1961, being created out of the television series called "Police Surgeon". The Avengers is one of the most stylish and successful television series ever made. Featuring the adventures of John Steed (played by Patrick MacNee), who along with his 'leather-clad' lady sidekicks, caught the imagination of the world. Today, thirty-five years after the first episodes were transmitted, the series still continues to thrill the world.

The first series also featured Ian Hendry playing the part of Dr. David Keel, who had set out to avenge the death of his fiancee, who had been shot in a London street by thugs. (Sadly only one episode "The Frighteners" still survives from this 1961 series).

The first female assistant joined in 1962 for the second series, when Catherine (Cathy) Gale, played by Honor Blackman, joined the fray replacing Keel, who had gone abroad on a fellowship. (Remember Blackman's Avengers spin-off hit single "Kinky Boots"?) Gale was "an attractive widow of independent means".

A cool blonde with a degree in anthropology, she was also required by Steed to display her prowess in Judo. Mrs. Emma Peel, a glamourous wealthy young widow, (played by Diana Rigg) joined in 1965 for the fourth series. With her sparkling wit, and a penchant for karate, sports cars and figure hugging black-leathers, (oooh) she was an immediate hit.

The fifth series in 1967, still with Rigg, was the first in colour. By now the 'thrilling' stories had become laced with a heady mix of 'tongue-firmly-in-cheek' and sauciness. The following year, Rigg left to be replaced by Tara King, (played by Linda Thorson) who relied more on her feminine guile than judo to dispatch her assailants. Miss King would use a coo or a kiss rather than a karate chop, not to mention an occasional 'brick-in-the-handbag' technique.

Miss King remained with Steed for the final two series. The final show of the Avengers, "Bizarre" was transmitted in 1969. Following moderately successful 'Avengers' stage-shows (featuring new cast members) in 1970, the series returned in a new guise as "The New Avengers" in 1976. This time Steed was ably assisted by both Joanna Lumley (Purdy) and Gareth Hunt (who played Gambit).

Keith, Mick & Brian with Honor Blackman in an unbroadcast episode of the Avengers

THE BACK COMB

Popular hairstyle favoured by the more flamboyant Mods. Hair was evenly divided in half across the centre of the head and combed in opposite directions away from the parting. This gave the appearance of wearer having a two tiered head. The style was taken to ridiculous lengths by Steve Marriott, and Roger Daltrey, but by far the worst offender was Mick, from Dave Dee, Dozy... oh you Know who we mean.

Back comb! Should have meant back to the barbers Tich, Beaky and Dozy were equally as guilty of offensive hairdos

Scoop of the season – the ELLIOTT thigh-high boot!

DAVID BAILEY

During the decade the fashion scene exploded and so did the requirements of a high quality professional photographer. These stunning photographs were considered the most effective way of projecting the current models of the era to the average teenage girl, via the glossy magazines. The top models of the day were without doubt Twiggy and Jean Shrimpton, and the man responsible for capturing their impeccable beauty and charm was none other than David Bailey. Born in 1938 in East Ham, London, his first assignment was as an assistant to the 'Daily Express' fashion photographer in 1959. He later set up business on his own where he secured a contract with the prestigious 'Vogue' magazine. It was during one of these sessions that he photographed Jean Shrimpton, turning her into one of the leading models of the Sixties. Eyebrows were raised when Bailey married his second wife, French actress Catherine Deneuve, in August 1965, the best man being Mick Jagger and the dress for all concerned being jeans and round-necked sweaters. Bailey was also the inspiration behind Michaelangelo Antonioni's cult 1966 film 'Blow Up', starring David Hemmings, Vanessa Redgrave and Sarah Miles. Bailey is solely responsible for the rib tickling taunt of innocent snappers being unjustly quizzed over thinking themselves to be the said "Smudger". He is also not beyond rubbing people's noses in the fact that his wife's a bit of alright seeing as several volumes of the nude Mrs Bailey are routinely available.

BATMAN

(ABC TV 1966 - 1968)

The characters of crime-fighters "Batman" and his side-kick "Robin" were created by Bob Kane, and making their first appearance in 1939, as part of "Detective Comics" number 27. However, for many (especially me), the colour 1960's American television series starring Adam West as 'Batman' and Burt Ward as 'Robin' was far better than the serious black & white 'Saturday Morning Pictures' show.

The ABC TV series first appeared on American Television at 7:30pm (EST) on Wednesday January 12th 1966 and on the ITV network in June during the hysteria that surrounded the '1966 World Cup Finals'. That week's 'TV Times' featured a story headlined "Batman Is Coming". The premiere show featuring Frank Gorshin as 'The Riddler' was titled "Hi Diddle Riddle", with the second part, transmitted one day later, "Smack In The Middle".

The episodes regularly ended with the cliffhanger "Same Bat-Time, same Bat-Channel" titles. Throughout the series, with its trademark ("Biff" and "Boff" amongst others) fight titles, the action was filmed using a tilted camera. The series was just marvellous! Even Robin got involved with his "Holy" Bat-Words such as "Holy Backfire", "Holy Cliffhangers" and "Holy Dilemma". Whereas, its predecessor was not funny, this 'modern-day' version was played for laughs, and didn't we love it!! The scrapes they would get into, (and out of), were so inventive, and simply so wonderful for this 'pop-art' era.

The merchandise spin-offs from the series were incredible. Psychedelic 'Penguin' and 'Joker' posters could hang

on your wall, and complement superbly, work by David Hockney, Alan Aldridge and Richard Avedon. There was even a wonderful Bat-Mobile model (in three different sizes) that could shoot little yellow pellets you'd lose behind the sofa, plus 'Bat-Costumes' that had no feet. The villains who attempted to outwit the 'dynamic-duo' read like a 'who's who' of the entertainment industry. Many celebrities felt that, regardless of their past achievements, they had not made it until they had guested on "Batman". The amazing cast-list of villains on the show included 'The Riddler' (Besides being played by Gorshin, was also played by "Addams Family" star John Astin), 'The Penguin', played by Burgess Meredith, 'The Joker' (Caesar Romero), 'Mr. Freeze' (played firstly by George Sanders, then Otto Preminger and finally Eli Wallach), 'Zelda The Great' (Anne Baxter), 'Mad Hatter' (David Wayne), 'False-Face' (Malachi Throne), 'Catwoman' (firstly played by Julie Newmar and then Eartha Kitt), 'King Tut' (Victor Buono), 'The Bookworm' (Roddy McDowall), 'The Archer' (Art Carney), 'The Minstrel' (Van Johnson), 'Ma Parker' (Shelley Winters), 'Clock King' (Walter Slezak), 'Egghead' (Vincent Price), 'Chandell' (Liberace), 'Marsha, Queen Of Diamonds' (Carolyn Jones), 'Shame' (Cliff Robertson), 'The Puzzler' (Maurice Evans), 'The Sandman' (Michael Rennie), 'Colonel Gumm' (Roger C. Carmel), and 'The Black Widow' (played by Miss Tallulah Bankhead, which was to be her last screen performance).

Due to dwindling audience viewing figures at the start of 1967, the producers decided to inject some 'sex appeal' into the series. Their solution was "Batgirl", played by the dancer Yvonne Craig. The character was introduced into the series at the start of the third season (in America) on September 14th, 1967, by which time the 'cliffhanger two-parter' had occasionally made way for a show which would start *and conclude* during its 23 minutes. Other new villains introduced during this third and last season, included 'The Siren', (played by English actress Joan Collins), 'Lola Lasagne' (Ethel Merman), 'Olga' (played by Anne Baxter who had previously played Zelda), 'Lord Marmaduke Ffogg' (Rudy Vallee), 'Lady Penelope Peasoup' (Glynis Johns), 'Louie The Lilac' (Milton Berle), 'Nora Clavicle' (Barbara Rush), 'Dr. Cassandra Spellcraft' (Ida Lupino), 'Cabala' (Howard Duff) and 'Minerva' (played by

Zsa Zsa Gabor) who appeared as the final villain in episode number 120 on March 14th, 1968.

A big-screen version of "Batman" was produced by 20th Century-Fox between television seasons, it starred The Penguin, The Joker and The Riddler (all played by their respective tv series actors). 'Catwoman' however, was played by Lee Meriwether, Julie Newmar was unavailable at the time of the shoot. The film, with a running time of 105 minutes, was released to the American cinema audiences on August 3rd 1966.

GEORGE BEST

Was he the world's greatest footballer? Debate will forever continue on that question. Was it possibly even Pele, Law, Charlton, Cryuff, Maradona? Whoever, but one point that no one will ever contest is that George Best was one of THE finest to grace the football stage, and at the same time, was THE first footballer to be treated with such fan worship. He was even nicknamed 'The

Fifth Beatle' due to his mop-top haircut. Modern day footballers (Paul Gascoigne being the best example) are poor comparisons to use when describing how 'big' George Best was in the soccer world back in the 60's/early 70's. He was admired by the press (for giving them something worthwhile to report on with his drinking escapades) the fans, who wanted to emulate his talents, (how many of us could not work out how he dribbled the ball, and got around defenders with such great ease) and, of course, 'The Mods'. Although watching Manchester United was not top of their fashion and music agenda, they viewed with great affection, the night-clubs he visited (eventually Best would open his own in Manchester) the stylish clothes he wore and the 'celebrities' he rubbed shoulders with. Not to mention, the extremely attractive females he appeared with on his arm.

Best, during this period, was everywhere. News cameras even filmed him waking up in the morning, with his dear Mum bringing him in a cup of tea! Best was born in Belfast in 1946, joined Manchester United as a 15 year-old in 1961, and made his first team debut in 1963. He went on to play more than 450 games for the club during the next ten years, scoring almost 200 goals. One of the most important was two minutes into extra-time during the 1968 European Cup Final at Wembley against Benfica. (Manchester United eventually winning 4-1, making them the first English winners of the trophy).

Best also helped United win two League Championships (1965 and 1967) but things turned sour for George in the 1970's, when following a series of disagreements with the United management, he left the club. Along the way he joined Stockport County, Fulham, Bournemouth, Hibernian and in America, he joined the North American Soccer League. His all-time low occurred when in the early 80's, he spent a short time in prison for tax evasion.

Whatever his behaviour, Best's contribution to the game of football has never been doubted, and he will always be regarded as one of the games greatest ever players. Sadly, we will not see his like again.

Best bits of Best:
His adverts for British eggs, The legendary implanted capsule in his stomach that would kill him if he continued to drink (it didn't work), the great song "Georgie, the Belfast Boy", his boozing and always giving Bobby Charlton the hump...gaw on George.

BEEHIVE HAIRSTYLE

A popular woman's hairstyle from the early 60's, so called because of it's beehive shape. This was created by back-combing (teasing) the hair towards it's roots, thus helping to create the required height. It was then smoothed over and vast quantities of hair lacquer were applied to hold it in place. Special back-combing combs were made available and these incorporated little nodules on the teeth. Due to the height of the 'Beehive' and another fashion accessory, the 'stiletto-heel' shoes, females were able to stand up to a foot more their normal height. Ridiculous press statements of the time inferred that the beehive title came about because bees (or even various insects) actually lived inside the girl's hair!

CILLA BLACK

Cilla was born Priscilla White in Liverpool, on May 27th 1943. She first studied at Anfield Commercial College, but it was during her association with The Beatles that her singing career really took off. She was first spotted in the 'Cavern Club' in Mathew Street, where she worked in the cloakroom. It was during a Beatles concert in Southport in 1963, that she made her first professional singing appearance, when she substituted for The Fourmost. She was spotted by John Lennon (who subsequently renamed her Cilla Black), and was immediately signed by Beatles manager Brian Epstein to his N.E.M.S. Enterprises stable of stars.

Her first minor chart success came in October 1963 with the Lennon-McCartney song "Love Of The Loved". Then in February 1964 she reached No.1 with "Anyone Who Had A Heart", a record which sold 100,000 copies in one day! She followed this with another No.1, "You're My World" three months later.

She complimented her chart successes with an appearance at the "Royal Variety Performance" along with her big screen debut in the 1967 film "Work....Is A Four Letter Word". In 1968, BBC Television rewarded her success with her own music series, simply titled "Cilla". The theme tune "Step Inside Love" was written by her old Beatle pal Paul McCartney. She later married her manager Bobby Willis in her native town of Liverpool. They are still happily married, where they have three sons, Robert, Benjamin and Jack.

Recommended listening:
"Anyone Who Had A Heart" (February 1964) Parlophone R 5101.
"You're My World" (May 1964) Parlophone R 5133
"It's For You" (August 1964) Parlophone R 5162
"Alfie" (March 1966) Parlophone R 5427
"Step Inside Love" (March 1968) Parlophone R 5674
"Surround Yourself With Sorrow" (February 1969) Parlophone R 5759

BLOW-UP

(Metro Goldwyn Mayer -1966)
"Hypnotic pop-culture parable of a photographer caught in a passive lifestyle. Arresting, provocative film rich in colour symbolism, many-layered meanings" was one description, "A fascinating and thought-provoking drama, involving a London photographer who believes he has witnessed a murder.....the film brims with psychological twists and complex symbolism" ran another.

Whatever you think of the film, you see more with each subsequent viewing. David Hemmings, influenced by real-life photographer David Bailey, is effective as the baffled young man, while Vanessa Redgrave gives a stylish performance as the young woman desperate to get the murder photographs incriminating her from Hemmings. Cameo appearances were made by Sarah Miles and a young Jane Birkin (who gives the first, albeit brief, full frontal nude scene in a major motion picture – oooh er).

The twist to the film, is that Hemmings is a 'Walter Mitty' type character, who by day works in the local factory and day-dreams of being a photographer. Subsequently, the murder and the characters portrayed in the film were purely an invention on his part. The only true event in his life occurs at the very start of the film, where he is seen leaving the factory clutching his bag of sandwiches, and talking to his workmates under the bridge. The moving images are possibly the best filmed example of Sixties London.

The film, a Carlo Ponti Production, was directed by Michaelangelo Antonioni with music by Herbert (Herbie) Hancock. The Yardbirds, featuring Jeff Beck and Jimmy Page, performed "Stroll On" in a mock-up of the 'Ricky-Tick' club in Windsor, Berkshire. Originally, the group had insisted on being filmed at this venue, but were told, due to space, this would be impossible. An agreement was reached when the producers told the group they would recreate the club on a film set at Pinewood Studios.

"Right, get yer kit off"

(British-Italian Co-Production -
111 minutes - colour)

Trivia note:
The park used in the film "Blow Up" is Marion Wilson park in Charlton, SE London. Charlton football ground is also the setting for one of the Who's finest live performances, where they were ably supported by Steve Marriott's Humble Pie (how's that for a tie in), and incidentally Marion Wilson park has a nice little animal enclosure which is lovely to take the kids to in the summer.

PATTI BOYD

(Mrs George Harrison 1966 -1977)
Born on March 17th 1944, Patti was already one of London's top models when she was hired by director Richard Lester (after he spotted her in a Smiths' crisps advert) to appear as a young schoolgirl on the train in The Beatles first film 'A Hard Days Night'. She met George on the set at Twickenham film studios. At first Patti spurned George's attempts for a date due to her engagement to another man. But his perserverence paid off when in 1965 she moved into Georges Esher bungalow home. Aside from her modelling work Patti regularly wrote for the U.S. teen magazine "16" called 'Pattie's Letter From London" concerning the English pop and rock scene.
On January 21st 1966 Patti and George married, with Paul the only other Beatle present. They honeymooned in Barbados shortly afterwards. Following the wedding, Patti went into semi-retirement, not wishing to capitalise on being a 'Beatle-wife'. She was later inspirational in introducing George to Indian Culture, and discovered the fashion and design group 'The Fool', who painted the outside of the Beatles 'Apple shop' in Baker Street, London. Due to Georges increasing devotion towards his goal of spiritual enlightenment, Patti was made to feel isolated and, in an attempt to instill jealousy in George, began a relationship with his close friend Eric Clapton. She and George seperated in 1974, divorcing in 1977. When she and Clapton married in 1979, George was an invited guest. "These pop stars eh!"
Patti Boyd (Harrison) has gone down in the annals of music history as inspiring various classic pop tunes, such as The Beatles "Something" in 1969, "For You Blue" in 1970, and later, "Wonderful Tonight" by Eric Clapton and most famously "Layla".

Patti Boyd, the original Patsy Kensit & Beatle George

TONY BLACKBURN

Born in Bournemouth in 1943 (his father was a doctor), Tony Blackburn become famous for his awful jokes (ie. "Why do woodworm like picnics? Because they enjoy eating out of doors!!") and the dog, Arnold, he made out he had in the studio (how sad was that). He first started spinning discs in July of 1964 on Radio Caroline and then on another "Pirate" station called "Radio London". (Of which Blackburn still describes as "the best station we've ever had in this country!") But on September 30th 1967, Tony found himself in the history books when he played "Flowers In The Rain" by The Move, and thus becoming the very first record played on "Wonderful" Radio One. Ironically, stations launched by the BBC to directly compete against the "Pirate Airwaves", on which Blackburn had become one the leading DJ's. As Radio One launched, Tony recalled his feelings in his autobiography. "On that day I was determined to be brighter and breezier than a hundred redcoats." By 1968, he was reported to be earning £60,000 a year. As the sixties progressed, he moved into television, where Southern ITV presented him with his own pop show entitled "Time For Blackburn". Then, also that year, the BBC asked him to become a regular presenter for the nation's top pop show "Top Of The Pops." But all was not well in his radio career, where his breakfast radio slot had now become the 9am slot, and by 1972, he was presenting the 'midday' show. By 1980, following more TV stints and even the occassional TV advertments, Tony took over from Ed Stewart in hosting the famous "Junior's Choice" radio show. This was followed by it's successor, "Tony Blackburn's Saturday Show." But in 1984, after 17 years, Blackburn left Radio One and joined BBC Radio London, where he presented a morning show for housewives, mixing a bit of soul with his trademark "naughty" jokes. This unfortunately lead to his eventual dismissal from the station, when bosses became concerned over his repeated rude remarks and stories. His notoriety saw him joining "Capitol Gold" in 1988 where he continued his recipe of awful jokes and non-stop chat, intermingled with classic tracks from the 50's,60's and 70's, were a perfect combination, and to this day, he is still much loved, respected and listened to. (His programme, basically a carbon copy of a show he would of presented on Radio One three decades ago, is aimed at nostalgic housewives, who, to coin a phrase, "grew up with him".) Recently, he even picked up the "Best Breakfast DJ Award". Don't we still love him? Yes... but not enough to print a picture of him, so instead here's some postcards that could have been sent to him, but weren't.

> **Best bits of old Tone must surely be:**
> *His emotional and tearful on-air breakdown over his wife Tessa Wyatt leaving him for "Man About the House" bloke Richard O'Sullivan "Now that was a priceless bit of radio" compounded by Tessa's blatant attempts at rubbing Tony's nose in it by appearing in bed with O'Sullivan at least twice an episode of "Robin's Nest", not to mention darning his socks... ooh Tessa.*

Flip side: Dear Tessa (no, we wouldn't be that cruel!)

The Kinks' drummer Mick Avery does some moonlight modelling

History has been unkind to The Birds, remembered chiefly for being Ron Woods first band and briefly for the publicity that surrounded their Birds verses The Byrds legal action and confrontation at London Airport in 1965. This was when the West Drayton modsters slapped no fewer than seven writs on their visiting US counterparts. The Birds claimed that The Byrds (are you following this!) had no right to use the name The Byrds as they had only been together for a year reaching number one with the hit "Mr Tambourine Man" had a hysterical girl following and knew Bob Dylan. Whereas The Birds had slogged it out in an old Commor Van for 4 years living on egg and chips released a minor hit, "Leaving here" and they knew Bo Diddley. The writs made

not a blind bit of difference to the Americans tour and both band kept a respectful distance. The Birds recorded four singles and released three of them on Decca before winding up on Robert Stigwoods "Reaction" label where their debut single was scrapped due to contractual wrangles, which would last a year. A single, "Say those magic words" did finally emerge, but the long lay off meant the band had lost momentum and saw their following tail off. The US Byrds stuck to their name and scored more major hits resulting in the English Birds changing their name to the even more confusing "Birds Birds". They appeared in a forgettable 'B' movie "The Deadly Bees" and recorded one more unissued single, "That's All I Need From You", but the long periods of inactivity and lack of recognition eventually brought about the disintegration of the band in 1967. Their bass player, Kim Gardner joined "The Creation" another of Stigwood's charges where he was joined briefly by Ron Wood in 1968. Ironic note, now Ron Wood knows Bob Dylan!

Group greeted with writs

WEEKLY POST UXBRIDGE EDITION

BYRDS V. BIRDS CLASH IN LOCAL POP ROW

"As far concerned Byrds were — they were prop

They're using our name - say locals

Classic Birds line up:
Ali McKenzie (Vocals) Ron Wood (Guitar and Vocals) Tony Munroe (Guitar and Vocals) Kim Gardner (Bass and Vocals) Pete McDaniels (Drums).
Recommended listening
"Leaving Here" DECCA F12140
"No Good Without You, Baby" DECCA F12257
"Say Those Magic Words" (as Birds Birds) REACTION 591005

The Birds perched atop elaborate Decca Records photographic props (see also Lulu)

MARC BOLAN

The "national elf" from Stoke Newington began his auspicious career, modelling Mod threads for a fashion spread in "Town and Country" magazine, as Mark Feld (his real name). As a face about town, he insinuated himself enough to secure a one-off Decca recording option, releasing a single "The Wizard', in 1965, which despite a "Ready Steady Go!" plug, promptly went nowhere. Despite (or maybe because of) an irrefutable belief in his own talents, Bolan (like his contemporary, David Bowie) continued to languish in obscurity. After a spell in Simon Napier-Bell's Mod shamsters, John's Children, in 1967, he formed a hippy acoustic duo with Steve Took, Tyrannosaurus Rex, but that's another story.

Recommended Listening:
"Just What You Want" COLUMBIA DB8124
(with John's Children) "Desdemona" TRACK 604003

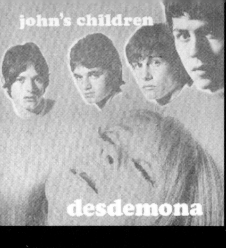

john's children

desdemona

BRICK RECORDS
549 005

John's children

Come and play with me in the garden

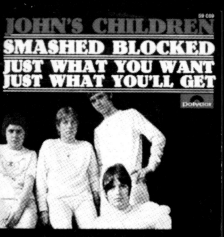

JOHN'S CHILDREN 59 C89

SMASHED BLOCKED
JUST WHAT YOU WANT
JUST WHAT YOU'LL GET

Polydor

John's Children
Go-Go Girl

Jagged Time Lapse

Polydor

Polydor 59 116

Come And Play With Me In The Garden
Sara, Crazy Child

JOHN'S CHILDREN

THE VARIETY CLUB OF
GREAT BRITAIN
WITH THE CO-OPERATION OF
REDIFFUSION
WELCOME YOU TO THE
READY, STEADY, GO!

EMPIRE POOL, WEMBLEY
WEDNESDAY, APRIL 8th 1964
7-30 to 11-30
OFFICIAL PROGRAMME
1/-

ALL PROCEEDS TO CHILDREN'S CHARITIES
THROUGH THE VARIETY CLUB

BALLS

The Ready, Steady, Go! Mod Ball was held on April 8th 1964 at the Empire Pool, Wembley. It was described at the time as the most ambitious outdoor event ever taken. It was the brainchild of Elkan Allan, the entertainment chief for Associated Rediffusion and the man responsible for the weekly TV version of R.S.G! He along with Francis Hitching, the TV show's editor, had decided to take its winning studio format on an outside live broadcast. Top secret plans were put into action under the codename 'Operation Mod Ball'. Bands booked to play were The Searchers, Sounds Incorporated, The Merseybeats, Kenny Lynch, Billy J Kramer, The Fourmost, Cilla Black, Kathy Kirby, The Dakotas, (Sad) Freddie and The Dreamers and Manfred Mann with the main attraction being The Rolling Stones. R.S.G.'s regular hosts, Keith Fordyce, Michael Aldred and Cathy McGowan would MC the event. A special announcement was made on the March 6th edition of the show informing anyone interested in attending the event to apply to the Variety Club of Great Britain for their £1 10/- tickets in aid of children's charities. 8,000 tickets were allocated (6,000 seating, 2,000 standing) and the audience were requested to attend the show dressed in "Bizarre mod fashions". All the tickets were sold out by the end of the first post on March 9th. With an unprecedented reply of well over 25,000 requests. The event, although a success, had its downside when a riot broke out between rival gangs of mods and rockers which left the Rolling Stones stranded on stage for 30 minutes while 30 arrests were made.

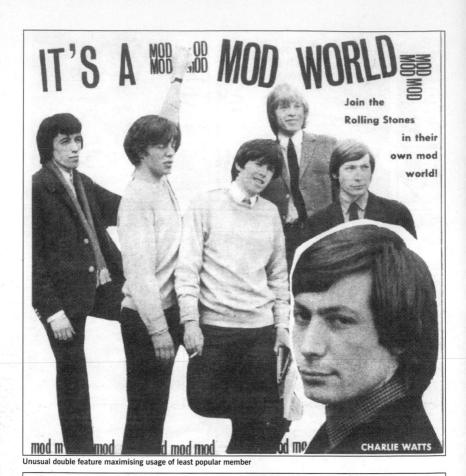

IT'S A MOD WORLD

MOD MOD
MOD MOD

MOD MOD
MOD

Join the
Rolling Stones
in their
own mod
world!

mod m   mod   d mod mod   od me

CHARLIE WATTS

Unusual double feature maximising usage of least popular member

IT'S FREE!!

AND
IT'S
COM-
ING
IN
BOY-
FRIEND!
A
16-PAGE
SUPPLE-
MENT
WITH
8 FULL
COLOUR PORTRAITS!

THE MOD BOOK OF THE STONES
BOYFRIEND EXTRA!

DRAMATIC

ARTICLES

ON EACH

INDIVIDUAL

STONE!

IT'S

PACKED

AND IT'S

ABOUT

THE STONES

ONLY!

DAVID BOWIE

Ha ha ha, hee hee hee

After releasing several unsuccessful singles on Decca and EMI Records (with the King Bees, the Manish Boys and the Lower Third), under his real name of David Jones, he signed to Pye Records in 1966, the same year the Monkees phenomenon broke worldwide, which catapulted another Davy Jones into the spotlight. Not wishing to compete with a manufactured Mancunian, he changed his name to Bowie releasing three singles on Pye before re-signing with Decca, under their subsidiary label, Deram, in late 1966. He released a string of stinkers that included the cringeworthy "Laughing Knome" and an album that claimed he was two years ahead of his time, but being too early is as bad as being too late, in the fame game and he was once again dropped, only to return, two years later, in 1969, from out of space, with a breakthrough hit, "Space Oddity". Bowie acknowledged his Mod roots in 1973 when he recorded the album 'Pin Ups' with The Spiders From Mars, which featured former Mojo Aynsley Dunbar on drums. It was a collection of Yardbirds, Pretty Things and Them covers dating back to Bowie's early 60's club days.

Recommended Listening:
"Can't Help Thinking About Me" (with The Lower Third) PYE 7N17020
"Do Anything You Say" PYE 7N17079
"London Boys" (EP) DECCA FR13864

THE BEATSTALKERS

The nattily betrousered Beatstalkers came unsurprisingly from Scotland. Although years ahead in the wardrobe department, they were sadly destined never to make their mark. Despite three spirited stabs at the singles market, twice with little known songs written by the then little known David Bowie: "Everything Is You" and "Silver Tree Top School For Boys" (Bowie had also failed with these songs) nothing else was heard of the group.

Trivia Note:
Bassist Alan Maivn went on to join The Only Ones in 1977 and had a hit with "Another Girl, Another Planet"

John Lithgow, second from left

Actor/Singer: Noel Harrison backing Britain in the US, 1966 with his customised Mini painted by Batmobile creator and customiser George Barris and featured in the 1967 american TV special "Noel Harrison goes to London"

CARNABY STREET

What was once a little known back street behind Regent Street in London, soon became, in the 1960's, one of the most famous streets in the world!! It became known as the centre for 'Mod' fashions during the decade, when shop after shop turned itself into a boutique carrying the very latest styles by the top designers.

During this time, the top shopkeeper in the street was John Stephen, a grocer's son from Glasgow in Scotland. At one time, he ran ten shops in Carnaby Street alone, including "Lord John", plus a further fourteen scattered throughout London's most influential areas.

The pop stars of the day were regularly photographed down the street, choosing the latest 'gear'. When two of The Monkees (Micky Dolenz and Mike Nesmith) came to Britain briefly in February 1967, they were happily snapped for "Fabulous 208" as they chose stylish clothes to take back to America. The Small Faces even had their offices in Carnaby Street (at numbers 52-55) as did the weekly pop paper the "New Musical Express".

Television crews from America were regular visitors to the street. One great example of this was when NBCtv in October 1966 filmed The Who driving down Carnaby Street in their jeep, with Keith Moon, attired in his Union-Jack Jacket, rushing out of a boutique and running to keep up with the vehicle. Also, take a look at the British films "The Haunted House Of Horror", starring Frankie Avalon and the Pathe News short, "A Look At Life" (both from 1969) to see how Carnaby Street really was in it's heyday.

Sadly, with the ever increasing onset of commercialism, the road made way for a public walkway, which meant you could no longer drive down the street. Today, Carnaby Street continues to pull in thousands of tourists on a regular basis, but the Carnaby Street we all fondly remember from the sixties, as portrayed through pictures and newsreels has sadly long since gone.

CHRISTMAS CLOBBER from CARNABY ST.

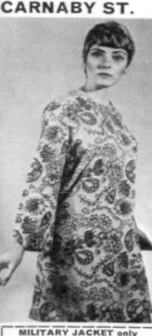

Radio Caroline, under the control of Ronan O'Rahilly, was launched in 1964 with one overall aim........to give top quality round-the-clock musical entertainment. The story began on Good Friday 1964 when the 'Radio Caroline' motorship, which was kitted-out at Greenore in Southern Ireland, took it's position off Harwich. That very same evening saw the very first test transmissions to the London and South-East regions, and the impact was immediate! Unbeknown to the station, listeners as far away as Glasgow and Bristol were also able to tune in, so it came as no surprise to find news of Caroline's unexpected existence had hit the newspaper headlines the following morning. By Easter Sunday, the transmissions from the ship had reached to regular all-day broadcasting. Not only were the newspapers taking notice, but also the experts of the 'Gallup' polls, who reported that, in it's first three weeks of broadcasting, the station was listened to by an audience of almost 7 million!! Then, six weeks after Caroline's launch, 'Radio Atlanta' (under the control of Allan Crawford) sailed in, dropping anchor some 14 miles from the Caroline ship.

Between them, the two ships aimed at, and reached, the second largest English-speaking audience on earth!! On July 3rd 1964, both ships merged under the 'Radio Caroline' call-sign. In it's prime, 'Caroline' was receiving more than 2,000 letters from fans a day at it's 'Caroline House' office set in the heart of London's West End. A number of house-hold DJ's made their radio debut on the station, such as the ex-wrestler Jimmy Savile, Simon Dee and the then 21 year-old Tony Blackburn.

The fairy-tale came to an end in 1967 when, due to the outlawing of pirate radio by the Labour government, the ship was emptied and the station went off-air. In it's place was the 'Wonderful Radio One' which was launched on September 30th..........

What was special about 'Radio Caroline'? In the words of a 20 year-old listener in 1965: "The announcers on Radio Caroline don't mouth glib show-business cliches, they don't talk down to us and they don't let too many words get in the way of the discs they spin. Above all, we like the unassuming and intelligent way they go to work..........we feel that each announcer is one of us." I don't think 'Radio Caroline' could have asked for a better definition of what it set out to do!

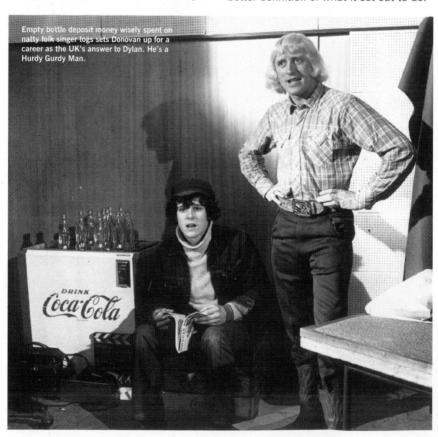

Empty bottle deposit money wisely spent on natty folk singer togs sets Donovan up for a career as the UK's answer to Dylan. He's a Hurdy Gurdy Man.

Below: Nerd-rock forerunners Manfred Mann, from left Manfred, Tom McGuinnes and that frightfully nice Paul Jones, keep their feet planted firmly on solid ground.

The Chocolate Watch Band take their cue from the Small Faces wardrobe for their '67 single "The Summer of Love". Oddly enough their Morris men shaky stick things would never again trouble the world of progressive rock.

THE CHOCOLATE WATCH BAND

The Chocolate Watch band got off to the confusing start of having to compete with the US group of the same name. Although the English version was easier to identify, being that there were only two of them, it was the American version that got the breaks, chiefly when they apeared in the cult film "Riot On Sunset Strip" or was that The Strawberry Alarm clock?

ERIC CLAPTON & JOHN MAYALL'S BLUESBREAKERS

The former Yardbird's brief liaison with John Mayall's Bluesbreakers remains for many blues and R&B enthusiasts Clapton's most magical period. It was certainly Mayall's band's greatest line-up giving prominence to the Skills of both John McVie and Eric Clapton. Along with drummer, Hughie Flint this line-up's self titled debut and Clapton's only album for Decca gave the label one of its biggest sellers of all time without so much as a hit single proceeding it. The album sleave with Clapton's face buried in the Beano is as famous a shot as any image from that era and according to photographer Dave Wedgeburry, completely spontaneous. "Eric just started reading the comic while he waited for me to set up the shot, I looked up from my viewfinder and there he was emersed in it, straight away I new I had my picture". Despite the album's massive success Clapton was to leave a few months later in order to form Cream whose arrival was greeted with a graffiti campaign throughout London which claimed 'Clapton is God' John Mayall remained on Decca and recorded a steady stream of brilliant albums while continuing his policy to promote the talents of young guitar players, such as Peter Green and Mick Taylor, throughout the bluesbreakers many line-ups. Trivia note: Jimi Hendrix' prime concern when considering a management agreement with former Animal Chas Chandler, was that if he came with him to London could Chandler secure a meeting with Clapton. The young American guitarist had, it seems, heard the graffiti read 'Clapton is good'!

Above: John Mayall, good judge of talent, bad at keeping it in his band.
Below: Grimstead keeps abreast of the times with this 1967 advertisement

Note obligatorily perched rock and roll style ciggy while E.C. does some last minute tuning uppery

John McVie

Top far left: Eric
Clapton during
recording of John
Mayall's
Bluesbreakers.
Bottom left: John
McVie.
This Page top: The
Bluesbreakers with
Clapton's
replacement, Peter
Green.
Bottom:
Bluesbreakers with
the American harp
player Paul
Butterfield.

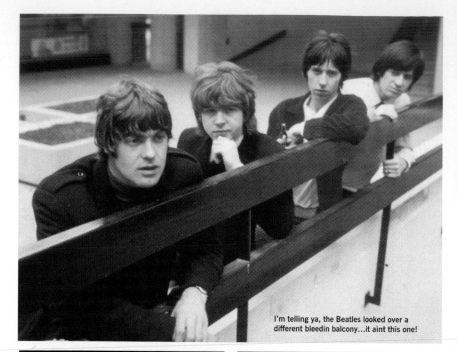

I'm telling ya, the Beatles looked over a different bleedin balcony...it aint this one!

THE CREATION

Originally called "The Mark Four", they changed their name in 1966 to the snappier "The Creation" and announced to the World their music was "Red With Purple Flashes". The bands debut single "Making Time" embraced the earliest aspects of that year's Mod/pop art trend being pioneered by "The Who", a band The Creation found themselves constantly compared to. "Making Time" featured an ear splitting guitar solo performed by the bands guitar player Eddie Phillips, using a violin bow a full three years before Jimmy Page. Their follow up single "Painter Man" took their Pop Art imagery even further with a live show that featured action painting by throwing paint bombs at large canvasses on stage and at the end of the gig setting light to them annoying local councils everywhere. More comparisons to The Who continued to dog the band and there was even a rumour that Phillips was to join their Shepherds Bush rivals. The Creation, despite front page coverage in the New Musical Express, were largely ignored in the UK and so concentrated on several successful tours (one supporting the Rolling Stones) and record releases rising to become Germany's top touring attraction. But constant personnel changes, which included the aforementioned Ron Wood & Kim Gardner from The Birds line-up, lost the band it's identity plus the lack of real hits especially at home meant the group called it a day in 1968.

Classic Creation line up:
Kenny Pickett (vocals) Eddie Phillips (guitar vocals)
Bob Garner (bass) Jack Jones (drums)
Recommended Listening:
"Making Time" PLANET PLF116
"Painter Man / Biff, Bang, Pow" PLANET PLF119
"If I Stay Too Long" POLYDOR 56177
"How Does it Feel to Feel" POLYDOR 56230
"Through My Eyes" POLYDOR 56207

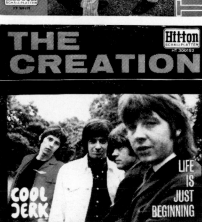

46

MICHAEL CAINE

Did you know that Michael Caine was born Maurice Micklewhite on the 14th March 1933 in Rotherhithe, South London - the son of a Billingsgate porter and a charlady. He changed his name after watching the film 'The Caine Mutiny' and suitably hooked on the big screen he went into acting at a relatively late age. He scored numerous bit parts in a handful of movies throughout 1960 - 62 before getting his big break in 1963 when he starred as the cheeky cockney chappie army officer in the epic 'Zulu'. He followed this success with a string of brilliant hit roles, most noticeably in the 1966 classic, 'Alfie' for which he received his first of three Oscars. Then came 'The Ipcress File', the first in a series of espionage thrillers where he starred as cheeky cockney chappie spy Harry Palmer.

Caine rounded off the 60's with what has come to be regarded by most as probably his best loved performance where he played cheeky cockney chappie bank robber Charlie Croker in the 1969 masterpiece 'The Italian Job'.

See also Harry Palmer clothes range

Recommended Watching:	
Zulu	*1963*
The Ipcress File	*1965*
Alfie	*1966*
Gambit	*1966*
Funeral In Berlin	*1966*
Billion Dollar Brain	*1967*
The Italian Job	*1969*

HOW DOES IT FEEL TO FEEL
IF I STAY TOO LONG

THE CREATION

Hit-ton
SCHALLPLATTEN
HT 300123

SHOES FOR YOUNG
WOMEN OF
TOMORROW

Clarks

DANGER MAN

Danger Man starring Patrick McGoohan as John Drake, first burst upon the ITV screens on September 12th 1960. The opening scene to the series began with McGoohan emerging from a federal building in Washington D.C., where he crosses to his white sports car, throws his raincoat onto the back seat and drives off. During this sequence, McGoohan himself narrates a voice-over, where he informs the audience "My name is Drake, John Drake".

Patrick was offered the role as Drake by the Australian born film director and producer Ralph Smart, after he had seen him in the television production 'The Big Knife'. Drake's role in 'Danger Man' was

as an 'undercover security operator for the North Atlantic Treaty Organisation' (NATO).

Over the next six years (1960-1966) a total of 86 'Danger Man' adventures (comprised within four seasons) were filmed. The shows, at the start of the second series, were extended from 28 to 58 minutes, and the very last two episodes in 1966, were in colour. Due to the 'espionage' angle to the show, greatly popular during the mid to late 60's, the show attracted a large following in America, where it was renamed 'Secret Agent'. In September 1966 McGoohan began work on a kind of follow-up to 'Danger Man', which featured a John Drake type of character in The Prisoner.

KIKI DEE

Born in Bradford as Pauline Mathews on March 6th 1947, Kiki first sang with various dance groups before recording her first disc "Early Night" (produced by Mitch Murray) in 1964. But it was not until 1968 that she recorded her first album, entitled "I'm Kiki Dee" for Fontana. But it was in the amazing feat of being the first British female singer to sign for the legendary Detroit based "Tamla-Motown" label, that she first gained recognition. Unfortunately, she failed to live up to the standards expected by such a great organisation, and was subsequently released from her contract. But help was at hand from friend Elton John, where he signed her to his "Rocket" label in 1973. In November of that year, she reached no. 13 with the track "Amoureuse" (aka "Loving And Free".) But of course, in 1976, she reached No. 1, dueting with Elton on "Don't Go Breaking My Heart". (Of course you knew that!) Later, she even had her own band, aptly titled "The Kiki Dee Band".

Five Studies in Colour of

SWINGING LONDON

Pick this one!
Kiki Dee
Now the
flowers cry

fontana
TF 983

SIMON DEE

Born as Nicholas Henry Dodd in Ottowa, Canada, 1935. He moved to England and was educated at Shrewsbury College. In 1964 he joined Radio Caroline and by 1967 Simon Dee was one of the most famous faces of the decade. His radio & TV shows made him a household name, but by 1970 he was forced to take up a living as a bus driver. Things got off to a great start for Dee when the Radio Caroline 'Pirate' DJ, jumped ship to present The Beatles with a 'Caroline Award' on the set of "Help!" at Twickenham Film Studios in April 1965, and then in 1966, he was invited to host the prestigious weekly top BBC1 pop show "Top Of The Pops". Due to the success of his appearances on the show (alongside 'jockette' Samantha Juste, who would later marry 'Monkee' Micky Dolenz) he was offered the chance of his own weekly chat and music show for BBC1, entitled "Dee Time".

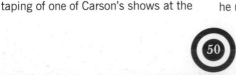

(Subsequently quitting 'Top Of The Pops' in March 1967 and 'Radio Luxembourg', where he regularly presented the Friday night programme 'Simon's Scene', to concentrate on the new series.)
Between 1967 and 1969, Dee hosted the twice-weekly (Tuesday and Thursdays) series, billed as "an early evening scene". At one stage, the audience viewing figures for the programme was totalling the amazing figure of 17 million per show. It's style of presentation for the show was influenced by America's top chat show host Johnny Carson, host of NBCtv's "Tonight Show'. (Hence the "Here's your host, SIIIIIIIIIIMON DEE" introduction, mimicking Carson's intro.) Towards the end of 1966, Dee was invited to watch a taping of one of Carson's shows at the 'Rockefeller Center', in New York City, USA where he sat nervously in the front row.

The premiere' edition (transmitted on Thursday March 23rd 1967) featured Lance Percival, Libby Morris, Mike Newman, Cat Stevens, The Jimi Hendrix Experience and Kiki Dee. The conclusion of each episode featured Dee in his open-top 'E-Type Jag.' driving around the BBC Television Centre in London, and stopping to pick up a mini-skirted young girl.

For someone so famous and trendy, it was natural that film roles would start to come in. In 1969, he was chosen to appear briefly in the Pathe colour newsreel "Look At Life", and was seen (albeit a cameo role) in the wonderful Michael Caine Gold-Bullion robbery film "The Italian Job", where he played the part of Adrian, the rather camp shirtmaker.

His first (and only) major acting role occurred in the 1970 Leslie Phillips comedy "Doctor In Trouble", (the last in the 'Doctor' film series) where he played the part of TV 'Doctor' Basil Beauchamp. Sacked by the BBC for allegedly 'upsetting the wrong people', Dee's meteoric fall to obscurity continued when he moved to London Weekend Television, where he presented his own late-night Sunday chat and music programme, simply called "The Simon Dee Show", which featured resident Jazz Musician Maynard Ferguson and his 14-piece orchestra. But this did not last for long, and Dee was forced to sign for unemployment benefit, and take all manor of jobs including one of a bus driver.

In April 1988, Dee resurfaced, as a promising new career in the media beckoned. But it was not to be, and he soon again returned to obscurity, where he remains to this day.

TWO

FOUR

SIX

EIGHT

TEN wheels with but a single tread . . .

DRUGS

Amphetamine Sulphate – Street name Speed/Whizz. Mods often took (and still do) purple hearts, black bombers, dexys and a derivative of sulphate to dance at allnighters often held in Soho. Many kids would come from the suburbs and stay in London all weekend. Dancing, shopping and generally living the 100% dream. Mods didn't rely on alcohol. They wanted to be on the ball not slumped in a corner like every other teenage cult at the time. In the late 60s and early 70s the northern soul scene took off with the help of the now legendary amphetamine fuelled allnighters at the Wigan Casino. the DJ's delved deeper into the obscure detroit labels and unearthed many Mod classics.

STEVE ELLIS (LOVE AFFAIR)

Sixteen year old apple pie faced Mod Steve Ellis's band Love Affair suffered Monkees style back lash when it was discovered that Ellis was the only member of the group who appeared on their records (the rest of the bands sound being supplied by session men). Ellis and his manager Decca Records chief smudger David Wedgeberry ignored slants of conning the public and recruited a band. They released a string of identical singles, which included Rainbow Valley, A day with out love, and Bringing on back the good times. The bands biggest hit and only number one, Everlasting Love, still stands as a timeless classic, and was covered in the Eighties by Mod five piece The Truth on their Five Live at the 100 club 12 inch EP, a title borrowed from the Yardbirds debut album Five Live Yardbirds.

THE EYES

The Eyes were a little remembered outfit that formed in Ealing in 1964 originally called The Aces then The Arrows which became The Renegades which in turn became Gary Hart and The Hartbeats. They settled on the name The Eyes (which was equally as crap a name as all the others) in 1966 in time to cash in on the pop art music movement being pioneered by The Who. The Eyes use the obligatory wail of feed back and distortion but combined it with a backing track of police sirens and sound effects such as skidding cars, alarm clocks and a little gong the drummer had bought for £2 down the Portobello Road which he would bong indiscriminately throughout their set. The group failed to have even a minor hit despite being the first band to advertise their efforts on railway hoardings and on 'London buses with the saying "The Eyes have it". They were last seen sporting London Underground uniforms which may have been a clue as to their eventual destination.

Classic Eyes line up:
Terry Nolder (Vocals) Barry Alchin (Bass) Chris Lovegrove (Rhythm Guitar) Phil Heatley (Lead Guitar) Brian Cororan (Drums)
Recommended Listening:
"The Immediate Pleasure" MERCURY MF897

Above: The Eyes, no taste, no style, no hit!

E-TYPE JAGUAR

See also Rickenbacker. We don't pretend to be car enthusiasts or mechanics, but we know what we like and we think that the E-Type was the ultimate British driving success. Also, all the films which featured E-Types were groovy and looked great, especially with the sound turned down, case in point being The Dave Clarke Five's film "Catch Us If You Can". They looked cool in "The Italian Job", "Get Carter" and the sureal "Prisoner" episode "The Girl Who Was Deaf" and Simon Dee's Jag made for a brilliant TV ending. But we can't know everything about everything so here's a picture of The Artwoods posing with their Jag.

Above: The Artwoods with an E-type jag. The group pictured before a tricky seating arrangement problem drove a wedge between band members whilst on the road. They eventually bought a transit van!

KENNY EVERET

Born Maurice James Christopher Cole in Seaforth, Liverpool on Christmas Day 1944. Originally, he first wanted to be a priest, but his first jobs saw him as someone who scraped "gunk" off the sausage roll trays in a Liverpool bakery. This was quickly followed by a position in an advertising agency before he became a disc-jockey on Radio Luxembourg and then on the pirate station Radio London. His nightly DJing stints at top Mod spot "Tiles" in Oxford Street landed him his biggest break when he was invited to cover The Beatles 1965 American tours for the radio. (Stories that came from the tour, Everett later admitted, were largely made up.) His involvement with The Beatles came again when he was asked to edit the group's annual Christmas flexi-discs for the fan club members. In 1968 he presented his first TV pop-show programme, entitled "Nice Time" for Granada ITV, and also briefly hosted "Top Of The Pops" for the BBC. Kenny joined Capitol Radio in 1973, and his BBC Radio 1 career (of which he has had two stints) came to a halt when, on air, he jokingly accused the then Transport Minister's wife, who had just passed her driving test, of "probably slipping the examiner a fiver!" At the end of the 1970's, Everett reappeared on Thames television in "The Kenny Everett Video Show", with resident dance group Hot Gossip and his wonderful radio character creations "Captain Kremmen" and "Cupid Stunt". Although Kenny, in his later life, made no secret of his homosexual lifestyle, he in fact married the singer Lee Middleton in 1969. He was to unfortunately die of an AIDS related illness in 1995.

lambretta ▼ 1st Class ticket to independence **lambretta**

LAMBRETTA to ANYWHERE

For conditions see over

THIS WEEK AT TILES!

'The Evening News' **"YOUNG LONDON SPINS"**	Star Disc Session introduced on stage by **DAVID WIGG**	**in TILES shopping arcade**
THE ALAN PRICE SET	**THE ANTEEEK** EVERETT OF ENGLAND	**LATE NIGHT SHOPPING EVERY NIGHT !**
THEM	**STEVE DARBYSHIRE** and **THE YUM-YUM BAND**	
THE RIOT SQUAD	**THE IN CROWD** EVERETT OF ENGLAND	
CLOSED FOR PRIVATE FUNCTION		
WILSON PICKETT EVERETT OF ENGLAND	**STEVE DARBYSHIRE** and **THE YUM-YUM BAND**	**NOW OPEN AT LUNCHTIMES!** Noon to 3 p.m. Entrance at 79 Oxford Street and 1 Dean Street
Radio Luxembourg's **'READY, STEADY, RADIO !'**	The U.K.'s biggest live radio show, introduced on stage by **EVERETT OF ENGLAND and DODIE WEST**	

Note the very modular monikered Everett of England

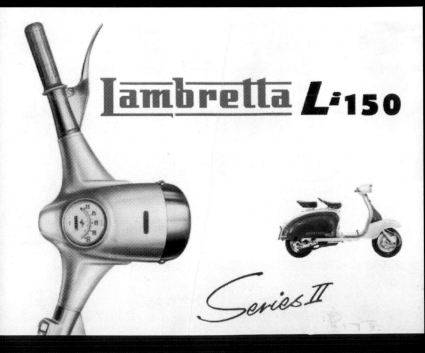

Lambretta L*i*150

Series II

MARIANNE FAITHFUL

FWithin just a matter of weeks of meeting Andrew Oldham at a party thrown by The Rolling Stones in July of 1964, convent school educated Marianne had recorded and released the Jagger/Richards song "As Tears Go By". Faithfull, was born in Hampstead, London, a daughter to the Austro-Hungarian Baroness Erisso, Eva Sacher-Masoch and the professor of Italian Renaissance studies Dr. Robert Glynn Faithfull. Her success with her first single prompted Decca to release simultaneously her first two Decca albums, something that was totally unique to the pop world. In 1965, she again reached the charts with her follow-up entitled "Come And Stay With Me" (reaching no. 4) and then quickly

followed this with "This Little Bird" (No.6) "Summer Nights" (No. 10) and finally, a cover of the Beatles song from their "Help!" album, "Yesterday", which reached No. 36 in November. Her final chart success was with "Is This What I Get For Loving You" which reached No. 43. Her relationship with Stones frontman Mick Jagger became public knowlegde from December 1966, and she became "infamous" as the "Mars Bars" girl following the Police raid at Keith's Redlands home in 1967. In 1968 she recorded the drug-inspired "Sister Morphine", even performing it in the long "unreleased" (until 1996) "The Rolling Stones Rock & Roll Circus". Unfortunately, her version never made it into the final edit of the film. In recent years, Marianne has returned fresh and extremely well, with her new recordings and her own autobiography.

I'll get some nice flock wallpaper for in here and some "nets"

GEORGIE FAME

Real name Clive Powell was early Mod favourite, heavily influenced by Blue Beat and Jamaican Ska, played great Hammond organ fronting his band the Blue Flames. He scored two huge hits with " Yeh Yeh" and " Get Away" before blowing most of his Mod cool by jumping on the 1967 gangster craze bandwagon, (along with the Artwoods, and released " The Ballard of Bonnie and Clyde". Trivia Note…. Fame was the first UK organ player to use the revolutionary split Hammond. Ex Blue Flame Micky Eves managed Steve Marriott in the 1980s.

George gets the Rave front page treatment amidst such viables as "Understand your animals" and potential blockbuster "Cathy McGowan's new hairstyle". Competition would never be so fierce

March of the Mods

MOROCCO BOUND
MARCH OF THE VOOMINS
GO HOME BILL LUDENDORF

JOE LOSS and his Band

EDDY GRIMSTEAD

G Scooter dealer from London's East End. He saw the need for customising scooters to order. Accused of being part of London's anti art scene. His scooters came with engine conversions, two tone paint work and ulma accessories.

DENNIS GREAVES

At a time during the late 70's when The Jam were turning on a whole new generation of kids to the genius of The Kinks and The Who Greaves' original 9 Below Zero were providing the same service with the blues. Dr Feelgood had just opened the pub doors to an un-catered for and starved R & B audience in the UK, at a time when progressive rock was a scorned dog of an option and punk rock ruled the earth. 9 Below Zero slipped in quietly behind them; younger, sharper dressed, tighter sounding and a sight more enjoyable. Despite sell-out venues 300 nights a year including the Hammersmith Odeon, in their own right, and support tours with The Who and The Kinks, a hit record would sadly elude them. Greaves went on to form the more soulful Mod 5 piece The Truth. They toured the US constantly and had two top twenty hits "Confusion" and "Stepping In The Right Direction" but unfair accusations of calculatingly attempting to fill the void left by the break up of The Jam eventually brought about the disbanding of the group. Greaves, suitably pissed off, found the blues once again and reformed 9 Below Zero.

Classic Truth line up:
Dennis Greaves (guitar, vocals); Mick Lister (guitar, vocals); Brian Bethal (bass, vocals); Chris Skornia (Hammond organ, vocals); Gary Wallis (drums)
Recommended Listening:
"Love a Go Go" "Nothing's Too Good For My Baby" "Exception of Love" all on WEA-Formation Records

The Truth! We're nothing like The Jam - there's five of us

No Rickenbacker or anything

THE "HARRY PALMER" FILMS

Harry Palmer, a character created by Len Deighton and played by Michael Caine in three feature films, was an unemotional Cockney civil servant turned secret agent. The first film was "The Ipcress File" in 1965. The plot concerned Palmer's attempts to track down a missing scientist behind the Iron Curtain, and discovering that one of his superiors is a spy. (108 minutes - colour) The sequel, "Funeral In Berlin" in 1966, features Palmer arranging for the defection of a Russian officer in charge of Berlin war security. (102 minutes - colour). The final film, "Billion Dollar Brain" in 1967, completed the trilogy, finding Palmer once again up to his roll-neck in exciting espionage in Scandinavia. (111 minutes - colour).

Horse Under Water   5'-

LEN DEIGHTON

Author of The IPCRESS File and Funeral in Berlin

Marriott with his reliable family run-about with sensible full AA cover

JOHN LEE HOOKER

The most celebrated Chicago bluesmen of the lot, he recorded under a number of pseudonyms during the 1950s but his heavy rhythmic boogie was unmistakable and he became one of the major influences on just about every white R+B revivalist from the sixties to the present day not to mention becoming the visual and musical influence for John Belushi and Dan Akroyd's Blues Brothers creation.

HAMMOND

The Following is the Top Mod One Hundred. They are in no particular order. Some of these singles were originally played in Clubs, Some have come to light in more recent years, Most of these records got little or no airplay on commercial radio.

1   1966. Tony Middleton - To the Ends of the Earth - Polydor BM 56704

2   1965. Dobie Gray - The in Crowd - London HL 9953

3   1966. Herbie Goins and the Night Timers - No.1 in Your Heart - Parlophone R 5478

4   1967. Shirley Ellis - Soul Time - C.B.S. 202606

5   1965. The Untamed - My Baby is Gone - Stateside SS 431

6   1965. Selectives - 1581 Rhythm Street - Uptown

7   1965. The Marvelettes - I'll Keep On Holding On - Tamla Motown TMG 518.

8   1965. Martha and the Vandellas - Nowwhere to Run - Tamla Motown - TMG 502

9   1966. Alan Bown Set - Emergency 999 - PYE 7N 17192

10 1966. Cavaliers - I Really Love You - R.C.A.

11 1965. Christine Quaite - If You've Got A Heart - Stateside - SS 435

12 1966. Garnett Mimms - Looking For You - United Artists - UP 1130

13 1965. Barbara Mason - Keep Him - London - HL 9977

14 1966. Edwin Starr - Stop Her On Shight - Polydor BM 56702

15 1966. Darrell Banks - Our Love Is In The Pocket - Stateside - SS 56702

16 1967. Eyes Of Blue - Super Market Full Of Cans - Deram - DM 114

17 1966. Temptations - Ain't Too Proud To Beg - Tamla Motown - TMG 565

18 1966. Johnny Saayles - Anything For You
   Liberty - LIB 12042

19 1966. Richard Kent Style - Go, Go
   Children - Columbia - DB 7964

20 1963. Major Lance - The Monkey
   Time - Columbia - DB 7099

21 1963. Guitar Red - Just You And I -
   PYE International - 7N 25219

22. 1964. James Brown - Out Of Sight -
   Phillips BF 1368

23. 1965. Marvin Gaye - I'll Be Doggone -
   Tamla Motown TMG 510

24. 1966. Gladys Knight - Just Walk In
   My Shoes - Tamla Motown - TMG
   576

25. 1966. Frank Wilson - Do I Love You
   (Indeed I Do) Tamla Motown -
   Tamla Motown TMG 1170

26. 1967. Barbara Lewis - I Remember
   The Feeling - Atlantic - 584061

27. 1965. Paul Kelly - Chills And Fever -
   Atlantic - AT 4053

28. 1967. Jackie Wilson - The Who Who
   Song - Coral Q 72496

29. 1967. Lee Drummond - Baby I
   Know - Fontana

30. 1966. Otis Redding - I Can't Turn
   You Loose - Anlantic 584 030

31. 1966. The Vontastics - Day Tripper -
   Chess - CRS 8043

32. 1966. Sugar Pie Desanto & Etta James - In
   The Basement - Chess - CRS 8034

33. 1965. Fontella Bass - Rescue Me - CRS 8023

34. 1965. Charles Dickens - In The City - Pye
   7N 15887

35. 1966. The Gass - The New Breed -
   Parlophone R 5456

36. 1966. Mose Allison - Young Man
   Blues - Prestige

37. 1966. The Action - Baby You've Got
   It - Parlophone R 5474

38. 1966. Googie Rene - Smokey Joe's La
   La - Atlantic AT 4076

39. 1966. The Capitols - Cool Jerk - Atlantic
584004

40. 1966. The Four Tops - Shake Me,
Wake Me - Tamla Motown TMG 553

41. 1964. Bo Street Runners - Bo
Street Runner - Decca F 11986

42. 1966. Kiki Dee - Small Town -
Fontana TF 669

43. 1966. Darrow Fletcher - My Young
Misery - Groovy

44. 1965. Sammy Ambrose - This Diamond
Ring - Stateside SS385.

45. 1966. Russell Evans & Nitehawks -
The Bold - Atlantic 584010

46. 1965. Chuck Jackson - Hand It
Over - Pye International 7N
25287

47. 1965. Nella Dodds - Finders
Keepers (Losers Weepers) - Pye
International 7N 25291

48. 1967. Spyder Turner - You're Good
Enough For Me - MGM 1332

49. 1965. Clayton Squares - Come And Get It - Decca F 12250

50. 1966. Billy Preston - In The Midnight Hour
- Capitol Cl 15458

51. 1966. Percy Milem - Call On Me -
Stateside SS 566

52. 1966. The Impressions - You've
Been Cheatin' - HMV Pop 1498

53. 1966. Sam And Dave - Hold On, I'm
Coming - Atlantic - S84 003

54. 1966. Bobby Sheen - Dr. Love - Capitol
CL 15455

55. 1966. Dyke & Blazers - The Wobble -
Original Sound

56. 1969. Georgie Fame - Somebody
Stole My Thunder - CBS

57. 1966. The Olympics - Baby Do The
Philly Dog - Fontana TF 778

58. 1966. Contours - Can You Jerk Like
Me - Stateside SS 381

59. 1965. Mary Love - I'm In Love - King
KG 1024

The Cryin Shames "Bloody ard up 't' north

60. 1965. Hit Pack - Never Say No To Your Baby - Tamla Motown TMG 513

61. 1964. Earl Van Dyke - Soul Stomp - Stateside SS 357

62. 1966. Albert Collins - Cookin' Catfish - 20th Century Fox

63. 1966. Slim Harpo - Shake Your Hips - Stateside SS 527

64. 1967. The Gypsies - Jerk It - CBS 201785

65. 1967. Mr. Dynamite - Sh' Mon (Parts 1& 2) Sue W 14027

66. 1966. Hesitations - You Can't Bypass Me - Kapp

67. 1966. Ray Charles - I Don't Need No Doctor - HMV Pop 1566

68. 1964. Fats Domino - If You Don't Know What Love Is - HMV Pop 1303

69. 1964. Derak Martin - Daddy Rollin' Stone - Sue W 1308

70. 1965. Twine Time - Alvin Cash - Stateside SS 386

71. 1968. Stay Loose - Jimmy Smith - Verve

72. 1967. The VIP's - Straight Downb To The Bottom - Island WIP 6005

73. 1967. The Spencer Davis Group - I'm A Man - Fontana TF 785

74. 1967. John Roberts - Sockin' - Sue WI 4042

75. 1967. The O'Jays - I'll Never Forget You - Imperial

76. 1965. Ray Pollard - The Drifter - United Artists UP 1111

77. 1966. Marva Whitney - Saving My Love For My Baby - Federal

78. 1969. Jimmy McGriff - The Worm - United Artists - UP 35025 (reissue)

79. 1968. Right Track - Billy Bunter - Soul City SC 113 (reissue)

80. 1965. Tony Clarke - The Entertainer - Chess CRS 8011

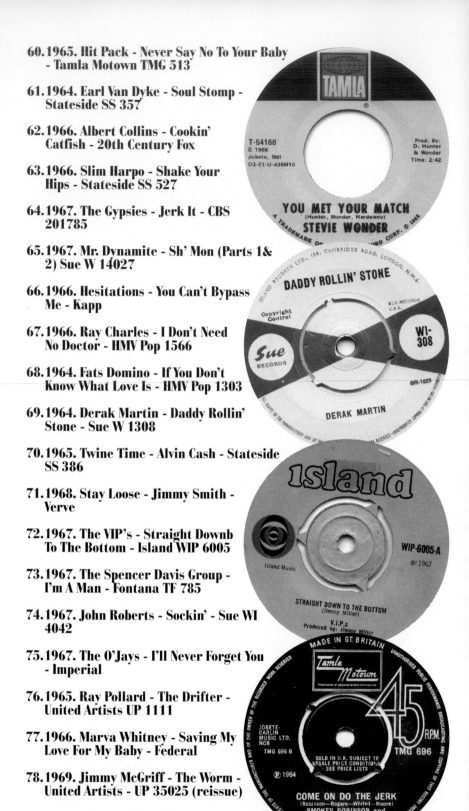

81. 1965. The Velvelettes - Really Sayin' Something - Stateside SS 387

82. 1966. Maxine Brown - One In A Million - Wand

83. 1966. Grant Green - Sookie Sookie - Blue Note

84. 1965. Baba Brooks - One Eyed Giant - Ska Beat JB 220

85. 1968. The Mowhawks - Baby Hold On (Parts 1 & 2) - Pama PM 739

86. 1963. Solomon Burke - Stupidity - London HLK 9763

87. 1965. Don Covay - See Saw - Atlantic AT 4056

88. 1966. Jackie Edwards - I Feel So Bad - Island WI 3006

89. 1967. The Quik - Burts Apple Crumb - Deram DM 121

90. 1966. Tony Galla - In Love - Swan

91. 1967. Dean Parrish - Skate (parts 1 & 2) - Stateside SS 580

92. 1965. Wilson Pickett - Let Me Be Your Boy - MGM 1286

93. 1969. Little Milton - Grits Ain't Groceries - Chess CRS 8087

94. 1965. Willie Mitchell - That Driving Beat - London HLU 10004

95. 1964. Betty Everett - Getting Mighty Crowded - Fontana TF 520

96. 1963. Prince Buster - The Ten Commandments - Blue Beat BB 167

97. 1965. Ketty Lester - West Coast - Capitol CL 15427

98. 1966. Lee Dorsey - Get Out Of My Life, Woman - Stateside SS 485

99. 1968. Clarence Carter - Looking For A Fox - Atlantic S84 176

100. 1965. Chris Farlowe and the Thunderbirds - Buzz With the Fuzz - Columbia DB7614

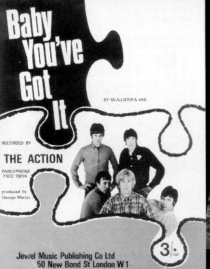
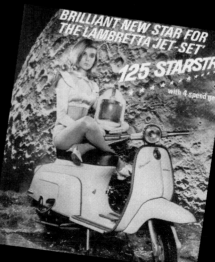

K

ALEXIS KORNER

The US have their Guv'nors, their Godfathers, and their Boss, but Britain has only managed The Daddy or in Korners case the Daddy of them all. Its a title openly acknowledged and respected with good reason by the scores of R and B-sters and latterday Rock Gods all of which owe their starts to Korner. Just some of the grateful include Mick Jagger, Charlie Watts, Brian Jones, Ginger Baker, Graham Bond, Jack Bruce, Dick Heckstall Smith, Cyril Davis, Zoot Money, and even Robert Plant who worked as one half of a duo with Korner before joining Led Zeppelin, Cheers Dad.

Beatles his and hers tights?

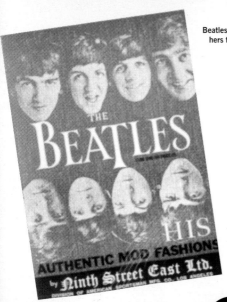

THE KINKS

The Kinks from Muswell Hill North London started there musical life as The Ravens with a sixteen year old Dave Davies at the helm. However it was Dave's older sibling Ray who proved to have the more natural singing capabilities coupled with a undeniable gift as a song writer. Discovered by manager and agent Larry Page who signed the group to Pye records in 1964 as the rechristened Kinks a name inspired in short by England's early sixties slang trend of describing every thing as Kinky, a popular term that even gave The Avenger's Honor Blackman the chance to release the single Kinky Boots,which in turn inspired the Kinks logo a kinky booted foot at the bottom of each letter of there name designed by the groups drummer Mick Avory's dad (trivial or what?). The band had two flop singles

the time, the one member who most embraced the Mod ethos, was Peter Quaife, whose favoured mode of transport, between gigs, was a GS (?) scooter. The Kinks scored 14 Top Thirty hits between 1964 and 1969 (including 3 Number One's, "You Really Got Me", "Tired of Waiting for You" and "Sunny Afternoon") and still continue to this day. With the current advent of Britpop, Ray Davies is now universally hailed as being the most archetypal of British songwriters.

Classic Kinks line up:
Ray Davies (guitar, vocals), Dave Davies (guitar, vocals), Peter Quaife (bass, temporarily replaced in 1966, by John Dalton), Mick Avory (Drums).
Recommended listening:
"You Really Got Me" PYE 7N15636
"Waterloo Sunset" PYE 7N17321
"Victoria" PYE 7N17865
"Lola" PYE 7N17961

When they open the door we'll all say we're from the gas board

before hitting it big time with their third "You Really Got Me" arguably the worlds first bona-fide Mod anthem, and the Kinks first number one record. The Kinks visual appearance was as immediate and fresh as was there irreverent approach to R & B. Page kitted them out in marketing pink hunting jackets, which were jettisoned in 1965, in favour of more casual mod wear. Although Dave Davies had outrageously long hair and clothes, for

SILVER BLADES ICE RINK STREATHAM

present **THE**
plus
THE **KINKS**
BLADES

ON MONDAY, JAN. 17th DURING THE NORMAL EVENING SKATING SESSION   DON'T MISS IT!   Adm. 5/6

DENNY LANE

Original sharp suited leader of Birmingham's Moody Blues (like Mod only with an extra O) who following their 1964 number one "Go now" were written off as one hit wonders. This is exactly how they remained as long as ole Den fronted the band. In 1965 taking the songs sentiments literally he left and wasn't really heard of again until joining Wings in 1972. Meanwhile his old band went on to achieve massive success with a load of orchestrated progressive tosh

RADIO LUXEMBOURG

For many of us, we all have fond memories of listening to Radio Luxembourg late at night, under the bed clothes (oy oy), with a signal that would constantly fade-in and out. With the shortage (before Radio One came about in 1967) of popular music on offer from the Radio, and the 'pirate' stations notoriously hard to track down, Luxembourg (or affectionately called 'Luxy') would be the station all 'pop-music' followers would tune-in to.

The station was founded in 1930, with it's original programmes (recorded at their London Hertford Street premises) transmitted from studios at the 'Villa Louvigny' in the Grand Duchy of Luxembourg. Broadcasting on it's 208 metres wavelength, the station would transmit nightly between 7:30pm and 3am. (Sundays would feature a 7:00pm start). During it's years, many top 'DJ's' came through their studio doors, such as Jimmy Saville, Jimmy Young, Simon Dee, Tony Price and 'BA' Barry Aldis, who regularly hosted the prestigious Sunday night "Top Twenty Show".

The success of the station spawned it's own weekly pop-music comic in the 'swinging 60's', naturally titled because of it's transmitting wavelength, "Fabulous 208". But all good things much come to an end, when in 1969, the station moved with the times, by stopping transmission on 208 and moved instead to a 'Satellite' radio station. Another example of a 'time-locked' period in time now departed, that each and every one of us share an equally fond memory.

LULU

Lulu, born in Glasgow, Scotland as Marie McDonald McLaughlin Lawrie in 1948, first found fame with her best remembered song, "Shout!" which crashed into the British charts in May 1964. This subsequently lead to Lulu being dubbed the 'British Brenda Lee'. She was reported to be singing by the time she first started to walk, and by the age of six, had won a talent contest in Blackpool. In1963, she was discovered by London impressario Marian Massey when she was singing with the group, 'The Gleneagles'. A recording session was arranged for the group, which had now been renamed by Massey as 'Lulu & The Luvvers', where they recorded the Isley Brothers hit Shout! It reached No. 7

Lulu with a more inspired use of the Decca box prop as supplied by Dave Wedgeberry

The Lesson According to Mod
Rielly remembers

So it came to pass. It was late 1963, on a Piccadilly Line train. I was somewhere between Green Park and Leicester Square when I saw him. He was standing up in his Anello & David cuban heel boots, topped off by a pair of Lilac bleached ankle swinger jeans, then a tab collar shirt with a crew neck jumper over it and a bouffant hairstyle which enlarged his 5 feet 5 inch stature to look about 5 feet 8 and a half inches. He was an early mod and did he look a Prince. Now my Dad was a West End publican at a pub off the Cambridge Circus called The Sussex and he was earning a few bob following the political cry of "you've never had it so good".

So I bought myself a Paisley Tab collar and black crew neck sweater and took off around Christmas time to see The Beatles at the Finsbury Park Astoria. My sister, years later, was to ask me, "What happened that night? you changed after that." What she didn't understand was that I'd found an identity around then, and I fancied myself as a mod.

So then, it was my first Tamla 45 by the Crystals and lots of visits to the record shop round the corner in McCartham Street to buy Prince Buster records on the original "Blue Beat" label.

Next step, was the West End niteclub scene where me and my mate Kevin Fenden got turned away from "Le Discoteque" in Wardour Street. The bouncer telling us we were too young. The real reason was that I just didn't look "Mod" enough with recently bought Italian shoes from a holiday in Sorreto, and a Trilby hat which was a poor imitation of a "Pork Pie Hat". Mod "one upmanship" supreme was delivered by Covent Garden's ace-face Jimmy O"Neil, when we discovered Hush Puppies had to be worn with red socks under your half-inch turn-up hems and Jim was playing football in his, having already broken in his second pair.

The clubs after that got to know our faces and we regularly visited places like "The Flamingo", "The Scene", and "Le Discoteque" which had a mattress on the dance floor for snogging. "Le Discoteque" also had a pinball machine where, if you got the highest score, you got a free entry into the club. I won it once, having tuned up in arcades all over the south east of England. In fact the Ace Face mod "Beardy Pegley" made a name for himself by walking into a Walston arcade and shooting a rocker. Stories about the local mods abounded and I remember Jimmy the midget who coveted having a scooter but couldn't ride one because he couldn't reach the pedals. So Jimmy bought a Lambretta and had a side-car fitted. The cops, however, didn't see it Jimmy's way and confiscated it!

Then there was the mod bands. I caught The Who at their Tuesday night residency at the Marquee and I can remember Keith Moon's awesome dexedrine induced drumming technique and Pete Townshend's flailing windmill style guitar playing. My mate Nozzie couldn't stop doing it all the next day.

"Ready Steady Go!" was popular on the TV and my old man regularly went apeshit when watching it. Now there were plenty of buskers who came into the pub and one of them was a feller called Donovan Leitch. He was regularly slung out of the sheltered alcove at the front entrance by my Dad after having kipped there the night. My old man used to come away saying "That's got rid of that lazy bastard". Then one night, Cathy McGowan on Ready Steady Go! announced the next big thing, introducing Donovan! My Dad slung his paper at the tele and went crackers, screaming "Donovan Leitch, that idle bastard, what's he doing on my telly?" He regularly went apeshit watching RSG! after that, including the time James Brown was led off in a cape screaming from the stage. That was simply too much.

I went to see the "Steam Packet" at the Marquee which featured a young Rod Stewart, who was calling himself "Rod The Mod". But the one I was really enamered with was Julie Driscoll, a love affair (or infatuation) that was to last until she did the unforgivable by marrying an "avant-garde" musician! Ponce!!

The old wardrobe was beginning to come along with Mohair suits, a blue suede jacket equipped with leather collar that I grew into three years too late. Pride of place though was a checkered Indian Madras cotton jacket which was truly, madly, deeply Mod! My regular mate Micky Evans had told me about a band playing down by the "Notre Dame Hall" in Leicester Square called the Small Faces. So we took off on one Friday and queued up. Then these two geezers turned up on the doorstep with the tastiest Madras jackets I'd ever seen. I got jealous and said to Mick "who's those flash bastards?" and he told me that it was the Small Faces!

After that, we regularly went down to the "Cavern" (corny name) to see the Small Faces in their original format 'til Ian McLagan took over from Jimmy Winston and set his organ up on me suede jacket.

Mod violence reared it's ugly head down there one night when a stand-in band played down there brought a following of "Hairies" with them. The hairies tried to take over the dance-floor and the mods mood turned ugly. I left just as it all went off and went for a walk down to the "Coffee Eln" where we dropped purple hearts and tore down the posters advertising the action, "the reason being?" I hear you ask. Well... we had seen The Who at all the little clubs when it cost a shilling to get in, then they got big and played bigger places which me and the original fans couldn't afford to get into. Then the same thing happened to the Small Faces so we felt we'd lost them as well, so we adopted The Action as our very own. Now we wasn't about to let the same thing happen to them so we'd go out, get pissed and tear their posters down, and you know what, they never did make it... and now you know why!

Editor's note: any members of The Action wishing to get in touch with Bill Rielly should send bribes to us at Empire Made and we'll put you in touch. All part of the service don't cha know.

NO MATTER WHO DRIVES WHAT...

WE ALL DRIVE **DAGENITE**LY!

Whoever you are, whatever make or model
of motor-bike or scooter you drive, you'll find
your Dagenite battery does a superb job.
It's tough, it's guaranteed, it's reliable and it's
economical. Rolls-Royce choose Dagenite —
can you do better?

DAGENITE MOTOR-CYCLE & SCOOTER BATTERIES

THE LONDON BOYS

A MOD MEMORY MAXI SINGLE FEATURING ORIGINAL 60's ARTISTS

featuring:
DAVID BOWIE
SMALL FACES
THE BIRDS
DOBIE GRAY

Above: Justin Hayward and John Lodge, Denny Laine's replacement in the Moody Blues. Left: London Boys EP, cringeworthily titled "A Mod Maxi Single" was Decca Records blatant stab at the 1979 Mod marketplace

in the singles charts.

Lulu and her group were in constant demand, appearing regularly on the BBCTV pop-music shows "Gadzooks!" and "Stramash". In 1966, she went solo and became the first British female pop singer to sing behind the 'iron curtain' in Poland. The following year, she co-starred opposite Sidney Poitier in the classroom drama "To Sir With Love" where she also sang the theme tune. Although never charting in Britain, the song went to number one in America. Rumours continued to flourish during this time of her alleged 'affair' with 'Monkee' Davy Jones, when the two were often seen pictured together in the latest 'pop-mags'.

Success followed success for Lulu, when also in the same year she was chosen to co-host the first colour BBC2 music related programme called "Two Of A Kind". By 1968 she was given her own BBC1 shows. The first being called "Lulu's Back In Town" and then, the following year, "Happening For Lulu". That same year also saw her marry Bee-Gee Maurice Gibb in Chalfont-St-Peters in Buckinghamshire and sing "Boom Bang-A-Bang" for Great Britain in the "Eurovision Song Contest".

Today, she still regularly appears on television and radio and even charted again recently. This time with Take That on the 1994 hit "Relight My Fire". Bit of an old Tory 'though, I'm afraid to say.

Recommended Listening:
"Shout!" (May 1964 Decca F 11884)
"The Boat That I Row" (April 1967 Columbia DB 8169)
"I'm A Tiger" (November 1968 Columbia DB 8500)
"Boom Bang-A-Bang" (March 1969 Columbia DB 8550)

AIMI MACDONALD

Hardly any British Television comedy shows in the 60's, such as "Do You Come Here Often" and the early 'Python' vehicle "At Last The 1948 Show", would be transmitted without an appearance, or even a 'bit-part' from 'Blonde-Giggling' Aimi MacDonald. Am I alone in thinking that Aimi's character was the inspiration behind Goldie Hawn in "Rowan & Martin's Laugh-In"?

Aimi was born on February 27th (year unknown) in Glasgow, but soon moved down to London in the sixties as her TV work increased, where she made cameo appearances in "The Avengers", "Man At The Top", and "The Saint". Also appearing in the feature films "Vampira" and "Take A Girl Like You". Her dumb-blonde character with a Mary Quant hairstyle, made her much-loved, and the 'swinging sixties' image of a 'Dolly Girl' made her a perfect choice when casting for TV roles.

She carried on her portrayal of this kind of female into the seventies, but as this was not the kind of image the 'Women of Today' wanted, her appearances began to dry up. Her last regular TV work was in the BBC children's comedy programme "Rentaghost" in the early '80's. Her proudest moments came when she appeared in the 1968 and 1983 Royal Variety Performances.

THE MAN FROM U.N.C.L.E.

One of the most compulsive, and stylish, American television shows of the 1960's was 'The Man From Uncle', a show hugely influenced by James Bond creator Ian Fleming. Testament to this is the wide range of gadgets, (a la' 007), used during the series. The show starred Robert Vaughn as Napoleon Solo and David McCallum as Illya Kuryakin. Their weekly exploits (transmitted in England on BBC1) as the men from U.N.C.L.E. (The United Network Command for Law Enforcement) concerned the battle to stop T.H.R.U.S.H. (Technological Hierarchy for the Removal of Undesirables and the Subjucation of Humanity) from dominating the world. U.N.C.L.E.'s headquarters were based behind 'Del Floria's' dry cleaning and tailoring repair shop in Manhattan, New York. The chief of U.N.C.L.E., Alexandra Waverley, was excellently played by Leo. G. Carroll. During the show's four year

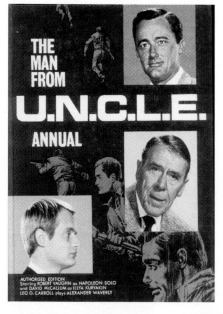

THE MAN FROM U.N.C.L.E. ANNUAL

AUTHORISED EDITION
Starring ROBERT VAUGHN as NAPOLEON SOLO
and DAVID McCALLUM as ILLYA KURYAKIN
LEO G. CARROLL plays ALEXANDER WAVERLY

(1964-1968) run, a number of well-known actors and actresses made guest appearances, such as Sharon Tate, Vincent Price, Joan Collins, Nancy Sinatra, Joan Crawford, Telly Savalas, Terry Thomas, Boris Karloff, Elke Sommer and even McCallum's then, real-life wife Jill Ireland.

Eight feature films of the series were produced, and in 1966 another 'spin-off' to the programme, "The Girl From U.N.C.L.E." starring Stephanie Powers and Noel Harrison (son of actor Rex) was made.

In 1983, both Vaughn and McCallum returned to their roles, with much lesser success, in the TV movie "The Return Of The Men From Uncle". With the tragic death of Leo. G. Carroll, his place as chief of U.N.C.L.E., was taken by Avengers star Patrick MacNee.

Recommended UNCLE films (with locations scenes shot in Europe:
"One Of Our Spies Is Missing" (MGM 1965)
"The Spy With My Face" (MGM 1966)
"The Spy In The Green Hat" (MGM 1966)
"The Venetian Affair" (MGM 1967)
"The Helicopter Spies" (MGM 1967)

DEAN MARTIN

Dino has been taken to the hearts of many Mods for all manner of cool reasons, he drank a lot, he played Matt Helm in a series of kitsch spy films, he hung out with Mafia nutcases in casinos in Vegas, he drank a lot, he was best mates with Frank Sinatra, he was Italian he drank a lot and well...he just drank a lot.

HAYLEY MILLS

Hayley was born in London on April 18th 1946. Her father was the well-respected actor John Mills. Hayley first took Ballet training at the 'Elmhurst Ballet School' and then, in 1958, made her film debut at the age of 12, appearing in the movie "Tiger Bay". In 1961, she starred opposite Alan Bates in the much-loved film "Whistle Down The Wind".

But it was during the mid-sixties that she really gained the recognition she rightfully deserved, when in 1966, she starred opposite Hywel Bennett in the film "The Family Way", which also starred her father John. Her part in the film was regarded by many pundits at the time, as being an example of the 'perfect housewife'. (Incidentally, the soundtrack music to the film was written by 'Beatle' Paul McCartney).

Hayley teamed up with Hywel again in 1969 to appear in the film "Twisted Nerve". (Incidentally, following the completion of the film, Hayley married Roy Boulting, one of the film's producers. She was 23 years his junior). Also In 1969 she starred opposite Oliver Reed in the film "Take A Girl Like You", where she played the part of a young girl fending off sexual advances from various men when she arrives in London for the first time. (Actually, the scenes where she arrives in London by train, were shot in Slough!).

During the decade, her face regularly adorned the pages of teen' pop magazines and comics, whilst at the same time, keeping away from any scandal. She was a classic example of the famous sixties female.

Her work on Television continues today, but she still retains a very private life, where she enjoys studying philosophy.

Trivia note:
Hayley Mills was also Mod slang for pills (Cor blimey!)

Lambretta

PERSONALISE
your
Lambretta

with genuine
Lambretta
ACCESSORIES

THE MAGIC LANTERNS

Caught out again, I'm ashamed to say, the sad truth is we don't know a hell of a lot about The Magic Lanterns. But if we'd left them out some know all would have raved about them, so we put them in regardless. What we do know is they covered The Monkees "Your auntie Grizelda".

Recommended Listening:
"Your Auntie Grizelda" (1967 CBS 202637)

THE MODS

Alright, we don't know anything about this lot either, other than the fact they were called The Mods and yes, that's why they are here when they don't resemble Mods in the slightest. Although the interesting one leg trouser affair (far right) was definately a fashion Faux Pas.

Recommended Listening:
"Something On My Mind" (1964 RCA 1399)

MOD'S MONTHLY

Short-lived cash in publication 'Mods' failed miserably after only a handful of issues. The publishers hopelessly misjudged the average Mod's notorious short attention span and their ever evolving tastes. It was a fact that Mod fashions and accessories could change overnight, often meaning what was considered 'in' at the beginning of the week could just as likely be 'out' by the end. 'Mod's' monthly turnaround meant it constantly found itself out in the cold!

MODESTY BLAISE

(20th Century-Fox Film 1966)
In what was her first English-speaking role, Monica Vitti played the legendary comic-strip secret agent. The film also starred Dirk Bogarde as the villain 'Gabriel' and Rosella Falk in the role of his sadistic assistant Mrs. Fothergill. Modesty is assisted in her battles by another classic sixties star Terence

PAN books X474

PETER O'DONNELL

Modesty Blaise

MONICA VITTI, TERENCE STAMP and DIRK BOGARDE star in an inspired and sensational screen version for 20th Century-Fox

Stamp.
Filmed at the height of the pop-art craze, it attempts to be a spoof at times, but doesn't know what it's supposed to be at other moments. Visually brilliant, the film was directed by Joseph Losey. (119 minutes- colour)

dial

Recording
First Published
1964
Dick James Music

DSP 7001 SIDE 1
V/7506 3

"SHE'S A MOD"
(Beale)
THE SENATORS

45 R.P.M.

"HIS MASTER'S VOICE"
MADE IN GT BRITAIN

MILLS
MUSIC
MCB

45-POP 836

7XEA 19984 45

SCOOTER CRAZY
(McHarg)
JOE GORDON FOLK FOUR

Tue. 1st	**MANFRED MANN** The D. J. Blues Band (Members: 6/– Non-members: 8/6) *Members' tickets in advance from February 22nd
Wed. 2nd	**CHRIS BARBER'S JAZZ BAND** with Kenneth Washington **RAM HOLDER BROS.** (Members: 5/– Non-members: 7/6)
Thur. 3rd	Jimmy James and the **VAGABONDS** **THE SUMMER SET**
Fri. 4th	**GARY FARR and the T-BONES** The Objects
Sat. 5th	Modern Jazz: **RONNIE ROSS QUARTET** **TONY KINSEY QUINTET**
Sun. 6th	**SUNDAY FOLK SPECIAL** Davy Graham, Max and John Le mont and Marilla Waesche (Members: 5/6 Non-members: 6/6)
Mon. 7th	**GRAHAM BOND Organisation** Felder's Orioles
Tue. 8th	**SPENCER DAVIS GROUP** The Explosive JIMMY CLIFF (Members: 6/– Non-members: 8/6) *Members' tickets in advance from March 8th
Wed. 9th	3 City 4, Al Stewart Backwater 4
Thur. 10th	**MARK LEEMAN FIVE** **THE SUMMER SET**
Fri. 11th	From the U.S.A.: **IRMA THOMAS and her Group** Roscoe Brown Combo
Sat. 12th	Modern Jazz: **DICK MORRISSEY QUARTET** **RAY WARLEIGH QUARTET**
Sun. 13th	**CLOSED**
Mon. 14th	**THE STEAM PACKET** Long John Baldry, Rod Stewart, Julie Driscoll, Brian Auger Trinity Target 66
Tue. 15th	The Return of **THE YARDBIRDS** The Clayton Squares (Members: 6/– Non-members: 8/6) *Members' tickets in advance from March 8th
Wed. 16th	**THE SPINNERS** New Harvesters, Mike Rogers
Thur. 17th	**MARK LEEMAN FIVE** The Objects
Fri. 18th	**DAVID BOWIE and the BUZZ** **THE SUMMER SET**
Sat. 19th	Modern Jazz: **DICK MORRISSEY QUARTET** **TONY KINSEY QUINTET**
Sun. 20th	**JAZZ 625** *(B.B.C.-T.V.)* Members only. Tickets available free on personal application one week prior to this date.
Mon. 21st	Jimmy James and the **VAGABONDS** **BOZ and the SIDEWINDERS**
Tue. 22nd	First appearance at the Marquee: **THE SMALL FACES** The Summer Set (Members: 6/– Non-members: 8/6) *Members' tickets in advance from March 15th
Wed. 23rd	**RAM HOLDER BROS.** Jo Ann Kelly, Shades of Blue
Thur. 24th	**MARK LEEMAN FIVE** Roscoe Brown Combo
Fri. 25th	**GARY FARR and the T-BONES** Alan Walker Group
Sat. 26th	Modern Jazz: **DICK MORRISSEY QUARTET** **JOHNNY SCOTT QUINTET**
Sun. 27th	To be announced Watch the "M.M." for details
Mon. 28th	**MIKE COTTON SOUND** with Lucas The D.J. Blues Band
Tue. 29th	**THE ACTION** The Loose Ends *Members' tickets in advance from March 22nd
Wed. 30th	**THE FRUGAL SOUND** New Harvesters, The Compromise
Thur. 31st	**MARK LEEMAN FIVE** Bo Street Runners

Every Saturday afternoon, 2.30–5.30 p.m.

"THE SATURDAY SHOW"

Top of the Pops both Live and on Disc
Introduced by Guest D.Js.,
featuring Star Personalities

Members: 3/6   Non-members: 4/6

(All Programmes are subject to alteration and the Management cannot be held responsible for non-appearance of artists.)

Nothing on at the Marquee again this month!

THE MARQUEE CLUB

Originally located on London's Oxford Street, the Famous Marquee Club moved to number 90, Wardour Street in 1964. The Marquee was the capital's premier music venue during its heyday in the 60's and was recognised as the breeding ground of legends. The Yardbirds recorded their debut album 'Five Live Yardbirds' there in 1964 and it was here that Eric Clapton aquired his 'slow hand' tag after repeatedly breaking strings at every show, he would take an age to restring his guitar and each time he was accompanied by the audiences slow hand clap. The Yardbirds continued to play ot the Marquee throughout their career, even after the original line-ups had metamorphosised into Led Zeppelin, or the 'New Yardbirds' as they were imaginatively billed, when they played their debut at the club in 1968. Other noticables who owe a lot to the club are undoubtably The Who, whose well known stark black and white 'Maximum R & B' poster advertising the group's righteous Tuesday night residency is one of that band's more familiar images. Bowie was another who first clicked with any sort of appreciative audience at The Marquee, mainly whilst supporting The Who on numerous occasions, playing in his Mod outfit, 'The Buzz'. He later acknowledged this period in his career when he covered two Who numbers 'I can't Explain' and 'Anyway, Anyhow,

Anywhere' on his aforementioned nod to mod 70's album 'Pin Ups'. The club consistently kept abrest of the changing music scene throughout the late 60's, 70's and the early 80's hosting many a London showcase for the likes of a fledgeling Genesis, The Jam and re-invented old mods like Status Quo and the ex John's Children spin off The Radio Stars. The Jam played their first Nom de Plume outing at the Marquee in 1981 under the pseudonym 'John's Boys' (geddit). This provided TV mod Gary Crowley with his first shot at music journalism when the Crow's revue was featured in the NME (trivia ain't in it). Sadly the club moved once again in the late 80's, this time to Charing Cross Road and in the move it seemed they forgot to pack the club's unique atmosphere as the new venue was a cold, soulless place that was never to present anything other than the most mundane of groups and little known artists.

Trivia note:
Other memorable recordings made at the Marquee include Eddie and the Hot Rods pre-punk EP 'Live at the Marquee' 9 Below Zero's debut LP 'Live at the Marquee" and the club's own Silver Jubilee series of celebratory albums entitled 'Live at the Marquee' (we assume). Seeing as there's nothing live at the Marquee anymore, these are essential listening.
*See also Beat Club Special 'Live at the Marquee'

MODS AND ROCKERS

1964 short film.
How many 'mods' remember seeing this extremely rare 25 minute short film from 1964, starring Hazel Merry, Peter Cazalet, Oliver Symons and the musical group The Cheynes? The synopsis for the film was as follows:
"A symbolic, ultra modern coffee bar sets the scene for a girl in gold lame' jeans, bolero and bootees, to start moving to the pulsating rhythms beating out from a glittering juke-box. As the music becomes progressively louder and more frantic, so the dancer increases the speed of her lithe movements to keep pace with the tempo. A boy starts to dance with this red-headed dynamo of a girl, but is repelled when she accepts the advances of a second boy. The two men vie for her attentions".

Top Mod designer, John Stephens previews his latest creation at his Carnaby Street boutique while a very young Angus Young, later of AC/DC takes the catwalk applause.

Trivia note:
Did you know that Angus' older brother was the guitarist in 60's Aussie rockers The Easybeats who scored with the number one hit "Friday on my Mind" (United Artists UP1157) also covered by Bowie on "Pin Ups". Steve Marriott would also record a track with the band on their 1968 album "Vigil". See that's the connection - small but noteworthy.

THE ACTION & EPISODE SIX

at the
CITY UNIVERSITY
St. John Street, E.C.1
(Nearest tube; ANGEL)
SAT., OCT. 21st (Adm. 7/6)

BEAT CLUB LIVE AT THE MARQUEE

On the 11th of March 1967, a camera team from "Beat Club" (German TV's Equivalent of "Top of the Pops") came to the Marquee to capture on TV a live show. This historic programme (The 18th in the Beat Club series) was hosted by Uschi Nerke (the German equivalent of Cathy McGowan of Ready, Steady, Go!) and from England - Dave Lee Travis and featured the following performances.

■ Cliff Bennett & The Rebel Rousers
   "I'll Take Good Care of You"
   ("I'll Take What I Want")

■ Geno Washington & The Ram Jam Band
   "Michael"
   "You Don't Know Like I Know"
   "Que Sera Sera"

■ The Jimi Hendrix Experience
   "Purple Haze"
   "Hey Joe"

■ The Smoke
   "My Friend Jack"

■ The Who
   "Happy Jack"
   "So Sad About Us"
   "My Generation"

(Thankfully, the complete show resides in the NDR Archive and clips - notably The Who and Jimi Hendrix, has been repeated on many occasions!)

THE MOD SQUAD

ASSIGNMENT: THE ARRANGER

AUTHORIZED EDITION

OLIVIA NEWTON JOHN

Commonly thought of as Australian, Olivia Newton John was in fact born in Cambridge, England (so that still leaves The Easybeats as the only Australian 60's act worth their Vegemite). She was shipped down under at the age of five when her parents emigrated. She first took up music as a singer with The Sol Four, eventually going solo in 1964 and winning a talent contest where she sang her later hit "Everything's Coming Up Roses". The first prize was a trip to swinging London and a contract with Decca Records (You don't get prizes like that on Stars In Their Eyes). Initial success eluded her until she joined the group Toomorrow, not to be confused with Tomorrow featuring the one-hit wonder and notoriously bad at finishing-things-once-started bloke, Keith West. Mind you, Toomorrow never had any hits, but it was the vehicle that certainly got John noticed when promo shots of the band showed Livvy displaying her white Knickers (phwoarr). She once again went solo and finally scored big time by taking the tried but tested route of recording and releasing the Bob Dylan number "If Not For You" as a single in 1971.

The Cryin Shames

Rhythm and Blues

The ART WOODS

SOLE REPRESENTATION
LONDON CITY AGENCY
REG 3378/9
189, WARDOUR ST. W.I.

ONE HUNDRED CLUB

The One Hundred club (known as the Hundred club) so named due to its address of 100 Oxford Street was primarily a jazz venue, although it regularly alotted an R & B evening one or sometimes two nights a week. One of the club's most regular residency holders throughout the early part of the 60's were the Artwoods. They played there so often that the band's retrospective 'Edsel' album, released in the early 80's was entitled '100 Oxford Street'.

100 CLUB

100 OXFORD ST., W.1.
7·30 to 11 p.m.

RHYTHM and BLUES

THURSDAY, July 2nd

GRAHAM BOND'S ORGANISATION

MONDAY, July 6th

THE MIKE COTTON SOUND

THE BLUES BY SIX

TUESDAY, July 7th

THE PRETTY THINGS

THE FARINAS

THURSDAY, July 9th

THE ART WOODS

THE T-BONES

Full details of the Club from the Secretary, 100 Club, 22 Newman Street, W.1. (LAN 0184).

Above and left: The Artwoods, Hundred Club stalwarts pictured everywhere but the Hundred Club!

HARRY PALMER OF LONDON

Harry Palmer of London was a range of clothes that was produced in the early '90s. All the items were based on the style and image of the Harry Palmer character played by Michael Caine in the films 'The Ipcress File', 'Funeral in Berlin' and 'Billion Dollar Brain'. The several collections made were a range of leather and suede rain macs, sports jackets, car coats, trench coats and various spy like accessories. There was also a prototype range of suede shirts. Unfortunately despite the patronage of such high profile luminaries as Paul Weller and Steve White, Kenny Jones (whose original Small Faces wardrobe had also been an influence) Ocean Colour Scene and Primal Scream's Bobby Gillespie, a major retail outlet for the clothes could not be found and the company fell apart at the seems descending into financial ruin.

"HARRY PALMER" FILMS

Harry Palmer, a character created by Len Deighton and played by Michael Caine in three feature films, was an unemotional Cockney secret agent. The first film was "The Ipcress File" in 1965. The plot concerned Palmer's attempts to track down a missing scientist behind the Iron Curtain, and discovering that one of his superiors is a spy. (108 minutes - colour).

The sequel, "Funeral In Berlin" in 1966, features Palmer arranging for the defection of a Russian officer in charge of Berlin war security. (102 minutes - colour). The final film, "Billion Dollar Brain" in 1967, completed the trilogy, finding Palmer once again up to his neck in exciting espionage in Scandinavia. (111 minutes - colour)..

Harry Palmer Clothing swing tag - the whole fiasco didn't swing!

FRED PERRY

The most famous tennis player from these shores. He launched his own merchandise company in the 60s. His most famous creation was the polo shirt, distinctive for the laurel leaf logo on the left breast. This is essential Mod wear for smart or casual. Later adopted by the skinheads and scooterboys. Look out for the green label Made in England not the Korean type.

I'm home dear

MARY QUANT OBE

Without any shadow of a doubt, the name of Mary Quant remains synonymous with the fashion boom of the 1960's. She knew what clothes young teenage girls wanted to wear. Clothes that could be classed as their own, and not something that their mothers would wear. (ie. dresses that featured a zip, that when opened, would reveal their 'belly-button') Although, contrary to popular belief she did not invent the 'mini-skirt', but she did make a large contribution in popularising it.

Mary was born in London in 1934, and it was during her time as an art student at Goldsmith's in the city, that she met her future husband and business partner Alexander Plunket-Greene. Together with Archie McNair, they opened their first 'Bazaar' boutique in the King's Road, Chelsea. Thus, with their contents of highly stylish originals, helped turn the King's Road into 'one of the fashion centres of the world'. A second 'Bazaar' shop opened in Knightsbridge in 1961, and this was followed by a large export deal with America two years later.

Her success was recognised in 1966 when she was awarded the OBE, the same year that her company (Ginger Group) moved into the lucrative world of cosmetics.

Her work is still recognised today, but more so with the range of cosmetics and textiles. Recently, she sold her trademark name to a large Japanese consortium, and has opened a new boutique in Knightsbridge.

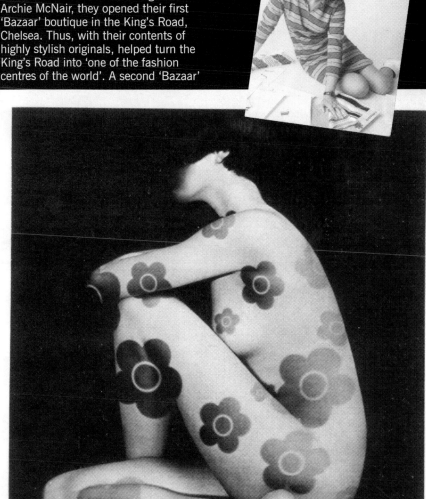

MARY QUANT GIVES YOU THE BARE ESSENTIALS

RADIO ONE

On September 29th 1967, as the BBC Light Programme, the Third Programmes and the Home Service, all waved goodbye to broadcasting, Radio One, as well as Radio 2, 3 & 4 all prepared for transmission. The launch day occured on September 30th 1967, when Tony Blackburn announced to the country "Welcome to the exciting sounds of Radio One". His first record was "Flowers in the Rain" by The Move.

The first Radio One DJ's, such as Blackburn, Jimmy Young, the late Kenny Everett, Pete Murray, Ed "Stewpot" Stewart, Bob "Blockbusters" Holness, Dave Cash, Pete Brady, (later of "Magpie", ITV's equivalent to "Blue Peter") and John Peel (the station's only survivor from day one) all happily posed on the steps of Broadcasting House in Portland Place announcing the arrival of the Beeb's new station, catering purely for "popular music". (The corporation later announced that with the release of The Beatles "Sgt. Peppers" in June 1967, pop music was now something to be taken seriously, therefore laying the groundwork for a station that was to become Radio One).

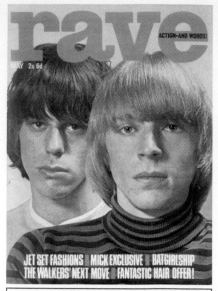

RAVE

Rave magazine began its shelf life in February 1964 after taking over from "Hit Parade" magazine when its 50's style popularity and loyalty to the likes of Billy Fury, Cliff Richard and Tommy Steele amongst others, failed to click with the 60's teenager. This failiure to move with the times in both its coverage of both the pop world and its colourful exponents gave birth to Rave. Rave was the ultimate teen music mag with a fornat to match mirroring the era's fast moving mod fashions and exciting times. Regular monthly features included DJ Alan Freemans "Heart to Heart" - exclusive interviews conducted on the rooftop of his London pad (with pictures always showing the Post Office Tower to let the reader know that fluff lived right in heart of the action - not arf), for example the October 1964 edition exposé on Jane Asher's life with Paul McCartney titled "How Paul changed my life" and the Small Faces in the July 1966 edition talked about their life while Sandie Shaw complained she never got anything she really wanted.

READY STEADY GO!

(Associated-Rediffusion/ ITV)
*Produced between August 9th 1963
and December 23rd 1966.*

Back in the summer of '63, just as The Beatles were whipping Britain's jaded music scene into a frenzy, "Ready Steady Go!" was launched as the nation's first foray into what is now known as 'yoof TV'. Prior to 'RSG!', music on television consisted of charming but uncomplicated programmes like BBC Television's "Juke Box Jury", which featured a format that still resembled the 1950's! But 'RSG!' came to the rescue. With 175 programmes spanning the next three years, and it's "The Weekend Starts Here" slogan, it came to epitomise the 'Swinging 60's', thrusting home-grown talents like The Beatles, The Rolling Stones, The Who, The Hollies, The Kinks and The Small Faces, amongst many others, into Britain's living rooms, as well as importing cool American sounds like Otis Redding and The Byrds.

With resident hosts Keith Fordyce (formerly of another ITV pop show "Thank Your Lucky Stars") and Cathy McGowan, you could groove to the latest 'modest' dance craze, pick up hot fashion tips, and generally make a fool of yourself in mime competitions. 'RSG!' went out at 'tea-time' on Friday evenings. The premiere' edition featured Billy Fury performing "In Summer" and "Somebody Else's Girl" alongside Brian Poole & The Tremeloes, who performed "Twist And Shout" and "Do You Love Me".

No artist ever made a fortune on the programme. For their rendition of "Bus Stop" on July 1st 1966, The Hollies were paid a handsome sum of £47-50 shillings, and for "A Girl Like You" on August 5th, The Troggs received 50 shillings more! The show often made pop history however: the episode transmitted on December 16th 1966 featured the TV debut of both Jimi Hendrix (with his 'Experience') performing "Hey Joe", and one of Marc Bolan's earliest performances with "Hippy Gumbo".

The final edition was transmitted, with an aptly amended title of 'Ready Steady Goes!', at 6:08pm on December 23rd 1966, featuring an (almost) 'Who's Who' of popular music from that time. Namely, Dave Dee & Co, Eric Burdon, Alan Price, The Who, Mick Jagger, Chris Farlowe, Lulu, two of The Yardbirds, Paul Jones, The Spencer Davis Group and Donovan, amongst others.

Sadly, only three complete episodes survive in the 'Official' Dave Clark (of DC5 fame) archives, two of which contain The Beatles. Plus many 'insert' performances and 'off-cut' clips (sent abroad, but never returned, ie. The Walker Brothers from 1966, which I personally found in German TV archives, and have since been returned to Mr. Clark). When Rediffusion lost it's franchise (ending it's right to broadcast on ITV) to Thames in 1968, the company moved into television rental and vacated its Aldwych HQ in the city of London. A cache of videotapes (then highly-prized for their reusable value), possibly including episodes of 'RSG!', were apparently donated to the up-and-coming 'Filmfair' company for them to record their new "Magic Roundabout" series on. The remaining archive was loaded onto a van, but spookily, never arrived at its destination. The old building has since become the registry for births, marriages and deaths; there's even talk of a cover-up in which the entire collection continues to exist, but is currently hidden away in a secret government warehouse- owing to its supposed inclusion of 'delicate' material. The entrepreneurial Dave Clark bought what was left of the 'RSG!' archive, apparently found underneath a stairwell of the old Aldwych site. Everything that has been seen on the PMI home videos and the Channel 4 (in England) and 'Disney Channel' (in America) compilations, stems from that hoard. But there is still much more that has yet to be recovered!!

A.R.TV's own R.S.G! magazine

RICKENBACKER

See also "E-Type Jag" for well ment informative and fascinating facts and once again you'll see we've come up short, we simply don't know that much about the subject. But once again we know what we like, and all that technical crap is boring anyway. However the Rickenbacker is without doubt the seminal Mod gee-tar par excellance favoured and championed by the best of 'em. So seeing as we can't tell you what the machine heads, stock finish, kneck or body are even made of, or why, or care, we'll list just a few of the "Ricky's" most famous patrons. With the Pewter punchbowl going for first place to John Lennon and his black ......for starting the craze, George Harrison in 2nd place for his Sunburst twelve string featured in "A Hard Day's Night" which was the influence for 3rd place Roger McGuinn to form The Byrds. Pete Townsend turned

TODAY'S MOST SENSATIONAL GUITAR SOUND

Rickenbacker

LISTEN TO 'BEATLES' JOHN AND GEORGE . . . THAT'S THE GREAT RICKENBACKER SOUND

In every important category—sound, appearance, ease of playing and dependability—Rickenbacker guitars lead the field.
They are made in America by the people with the longest experience in the manufacture of professional quality electronic guitars. Every Rickenbacker feature is an outstanding achievement in engineering and structural craftsmanship—a better instrument—to produce better sound.
Professional guitarists interpret the Rickenbacker superiority into greater playing accomplishment. It is a partnership of technical and artistic talent offering horizons of unlimited accomplishment.

Rose, Morris
SPONSORED INSTRUMENTS

the Rickenbacker into a Who trademark in the mid 60's while Paul Weller made it his own in late 70's England leaving Tom Petty to cover for the States.

Opposite page: Pete Townsend
This page top: Paul Weller
Above: Hilton Valentine of The Animals
Right: Billy Hassett of 79's finest, The Chords
Below: Pete Townsend again

THE SAINT

(starring Roger Moore. ITC 1962 - 1969)

Although the 'The Saint' had been common place since 1938 by way of the cinema, where nine films made. (The fourth in the series was "The Saint's Double Trouble" in 1940, with George Sanders playing the lead.) The character also appeared in various radio and comic strips, but it was not until 1962 that the character, created by Leslie Charteris, first appeared in a Television production.

The man chosen to play the role of the suave, smooth-talking character of Simon Templar was Roger Moore, who had previously been in such television roles as 'Ivanhoe' and as cousin Beau in the western serial 'Maverick'. (Ironically, Moore was the original choice to play James Bond in 1962, a role he would eventually take in 1973, but declined the offer due to his agreement to star in The Saint.) Templar was a private detective and his exploits were often to the annoyance of Scotland Yard's Superintendent Claude Teal. Usually because Templar would solve the mysteries before Teal's men could even get to the bottom of them. The first episode, entitled "The Talented

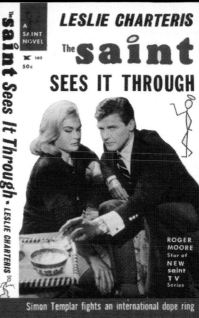

LESLIE CHARTERIS
A SAINT NOVEL
K 102 50c
The **saint**
SEES IT THROUGH

'The saint Sees It Through' - LESLIE CHARTERIS

ROGER MOORE
Star of
NEW
saint
T V
Series

Simon Templar fights an international dope ring

Right: Roger Moore presents a trophy to Miss Vespa 1965. Below: The Saint poses with his famous Volvo, which he (Roger Moore) incidentally bought from his friend, the sinister looking British character actor, Martin Benson who also played the part of the original character Napoleon Solo in the Bond film Goldfinger. Solo's character was later given an overhaul and changed from vicious mobster to suave spy in "The Man From U.N.C.L.E.'

Husband", appeared on ITV on October 4th 1962. With a bevy of beautiful girls by his side, The Saint, would be seen jetting off to all destinations of the globe, foiling murderers, jewel thieves and terrorists, amongst many others. His trademark was the Volvo two-seater sports car which carried the registration number "ST1". In total, 118 episodes (in six series) were produced between 1962 and 1969, the last two being in colour. The series was sold to over 100 countries around the world.

The series returned in 1978 as "The Return Of The Saint", with Ian Ogilvy playing the part of Simon Templar. This time, his trademark Volvo was replaced by a Jaguar XJS.

(EARLY) STATUS QUO

The first (and best) line-up featured Francis Rossi (born Francis Dominic Rossi on April 29th 1949 in Forest Hill, London) on guitar, Rob Lynes (born on October 25th 1943 in Redhill, Surrey), Rick Parfitt (born Richard Harrison on October 12th 1948 in Woking, Surrey), Alan Lancaster (born February 7th 1949 in Peckham, London) and John Coghlan (born September 19th 1946 in Dulwich, London).

The group make their live debut at the Samuel Jones sports club in 1962 where they call themselves The Spectres. The group continued to play working men's clubs for two years until a gas fitter by

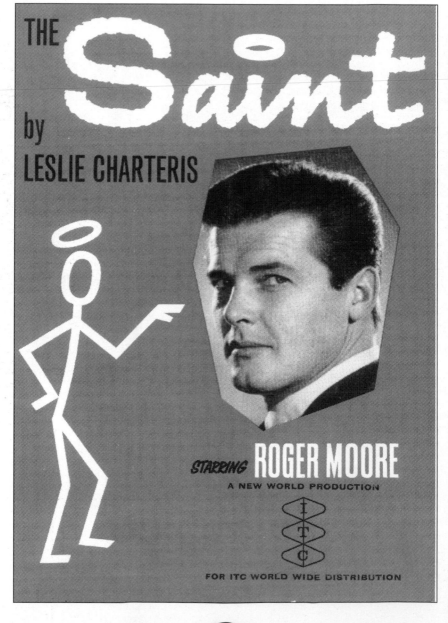

THE **Saint**

by **LESLIE CHARTERIS**

STARRING **ROGER MOORE**

A NEW WORLD PRODUCTION

FOR ITC WORLD WIDE DISTRIBUTION

the name of Pat Barlow offers to manage them and gives them a Monday night residency at the Cafe des Artists in London's Brompton Road. He also arranges for them to play a gig with The Hollies. In 1965 they accept a four month contract at Butlins. In July 1966, Ronnie Scott introduces the group to 'Pye Records' recording manager John Schroeder. The group sign to Piccadilly, licensed to Pye. In September, the group released their first single entitled "I (Who Have Nothing)". (The single fails to chart.)

The next single, again a flop, is "Hurdy Gurdy Man". After another flop single, the aptly titled, "We Ain't Got Nothin' Yet" in February of 1967, the group change their name to Traffic Jam, where they release the album titled "Almost But Not Quite There", about the same time as Steve Winwood leaves The Spencer Davis Group and forms Traffic. Their manager Pat Barlow, suggests another name change, this time Status Quo. The group signs to the 'Pye' label.

With the group now working as Madeline Bell's backing group, the band's first release on the label is "Pictures Of Matchstick Men" in February 1968. On April 5th of that year, the group undertake a 28 date UK tour with Gene Pitney, Amen Corner, Don Partridge, Simon Dupree & The Big Sound amongst others. On March 16th 1969 the group's first US tour opens in Philadelphia, PA. But by October of that year, the group waved goodbye to their stylish 'Mod' clothes and neat haircuts when they became more progressive and their sound more heavier and funkier and their hair alot more longer.

Today, they are still actively touring, (15 years after their farewell shows!) but sadly, they do not resemble the great act they once were. Only Rossi and Parfitt remain from the brilliant line-up we had in the 60's and 70's. Two years ago, in 1995, they returned to 'Butlins' for a thirtieth anniversary concert.

Top: Waterproof scooter coats from Mendac. Various labels clockwise: Unreleased acetate "Mystery" - the single was due for release in Oct 1966, complete with hole in the centre. A really, really rare version of "My Mind's Eye" which replaced it, with an even bigger hole. A really, really, really rare acetate of "What 'cha Gonna do About It" with (collector's note) a similar hole to "Mystery". A not so really, really rare "Tin Soldier", note the running time of 2:76 seconds! (And a far more elaborate hole.)

SWEAT SHIRTS

The humble sweat shirt was an unbelievably hard-to-find item in the early 60's and custom made ones caused a small fashion revolution. The big trend started following the British invasion of the US when visiting bands were given promotional sweat shirts from the American radio stations they visited. Unfortunately it seems that all the groups dropped in at all the same stations causing many a red faced encounter at the departure lounge!

Below: The Animals with Eric Burdon
Right: Rave girl filling out her sweatshirt rather better than Eric did

Left: Peter Noone, and top: The Nashville Teens, both in the 60's. Above: Acid Jazz band Corduroy in the 90's proving that careful washing can prolong the life of a sweatshirt's motif

To distance themselves even further from conventional uniformity the Mods adopted Vespa & Lambretta scooters to take them wherever they desired, without having to rub shoulders with the public. The bond between Mods and scooters was an obvious one. They were easily available at the time when h.p. was making its debut. Weekly payments made it even easier to own a brand new steel tubular frame with everything else fitted around it. The engine was centrally mounted but less accessible than the Vespa. Plus many of its parts were interchangeable throughout the range of models. This makes it very difficult to buy a genuine TV200 in its original state although to the untrained eye it would look sound.

Mods weren't the only people to own scooters in 1965 there were more

machine. Scooters had been made since the mid forties when Italy (funded with American money) rebuilt factories gutted in the allied bombings and used its engineering skills to get the country moving again. It took some years before they reached Britain's shores. Being Italian, they gave the scooter an appeal the Mods loved - sleek lines and bosom like curves (Oo er). Customising scooters was made easily by the amount of chrome accessories available at the time, giving the Mods an even greater individuality within the scene. You would often have some insignia written on your flyscreen like the rider's name and London postcode, e.g. "Dave SE London". Also, the riders were told, scooters gave weather protection via their legshields. This of course was rubbish, and as well as offering little or no protection against the elements they were also very difficult to ride competently. The Vespa's engine was to the right of centre hidden by a bubble (panel). This leads to difficulties when cornering in the wet. The Lambretta was a totally different design to the Vespa. The chassis consisted of a scooters sold in the UK than motorcycles!! There are many stories of Mods stealing scooters from other areas to use the parts for their own. Security wasn't deemed an important factor

scooter available clocking up an impressive 75 mph. Most accessories on Lambrettas added a different dimension to the bike, unlike Vespas where they accentuate the curves. Unfortunately Lambrettas vibrate and anything bolted to them eventually falls off. In the latter part of the 60's the performance war hotted up between Vespa and Lambretta. Vespa introduced the SS120 and Lambretta the SX200. Retailers saw the need for customisation and added extra chrome work and new ranges of accessories giving rise to larger installments on their hire purchase schemes.

then. The same ignition key started all Vespa GSs made between 1956 and 1965!! This made it even cheaper to replace and maintain machines.

The Vespa GS160 MkII was the ultimate London Mod machine available for only three years between '63 and '65. It had a spare wheel and large glove box which slotted onto the inside of the leg shields. It come in only one colour - white with aluminium strips on the panels and mudguards. Mods would paint a section of the mudguards and panels in order to give the scooter a two tone effect, favoured colours were British racing green, midnight blue and red. Accessories such as Jag lights were added to the panels and these incorporated extra stop and parking lights. New Yorkers and Florida bars would hug the panels and give the rider invaluable protection were he to drop the machine. A front rack would often be added adorned with lights, mirrors and alpine horns, all these extras would slow the bike down considerably, although this didn't bother Mods as speed wasn't their priority, the slower you go, the more people see you.

The Lambretta most favoured by Mods was the TV200, this was a sleek almost rocket shaped scooter. Lambretta had had the foresight to offer their bikes with different coloured panels from standard, painted mudguards and leg shields. The panels would fit flat and had two knuckle closers and aluminium flashes fixed to them, this gave the impression the scooter was moving even when stationery. The TV200 was the fastest

SCOOTERS - BACKGROUND

The hey day of the scooter was really the fifties in terms of mass appeal, though the mod association means that scooters tend to be remembered-in Britain at least- as a sixties item. In Britain-as elsewhere- rising living standards resulting in increased car ownership meant that scooter sales had already peaked by the time mod came into being, and quite a few dealers had already closed down. Although there had been literally dozens of makes of scooter, there were really only two that merited serious consideration-Vespa and Lambretta. In their native Italy, and most other countries, the Vespa was the most popular of the two. It Britain the situation was different. The Lambretta was imported by the Agg family, who embarked upon a dynamic marketing campaign that overshadowed that of Douglas, who both built and imported Vespas. The result was more Lambretta dealers and therefore more Lambretta sales.

There were plenty of things to attract mods to scooters. Firstly there was the styling which was modern and streamlined and complimented the look of the mod image. Secondly the enclosed bodywork allowed normal clothes to be worn, unlike a motorbike which tended to cover the trousers of its rider with grease.

A third reason was the willingness of dealers to arrange credit terms which included insurance - not every finance or insurance broker would welcome a sixteen year old as a client. Scooters had a good reputation for reliability which was important to mods who had far better things to do than get their hands dirty with mechanical repairs. Mind you, this was before the trend to increase power by fitting enlarged cylinder barrels came along.

Dozy, Sleepy, Sneezy & Doc, Carnaby Street 1966.

TYPES OF SCOOTER

Two commonly asked questions are 'what was the best scooter?', and 'which were the top mod scooters?'

The second question is easily answered. Two essential ingredients of mod were being flash and being up to date. Consequently the latest top-of-the-range models from Vespa and Lambretta were considered to be the top scooters - no other make was worth considering.

At the very beginning of mod the top scooters were the GS150 and the TV175 series two. These were replaced in 1962 by the GS160 and TV175 series three. The latter was replaced by the GT200 in 1963, which in turn was succeeded by the SX200 in 1966. The GS160 was replaced during 1965 by the SS180. All of these can stake a claim to being the "top Mod scooter", but it can fairly be said that during the peak period of mod the GS160 and GT200 were the ones to have.

As to the first question, then, as now, there was endless debate as to the relative merits of Vespa and Lambretta. The reality was that decisions on purchase were rarely made on the basis of an objective assessment of technical merit. A sixteen year old mod would tend to buy whatever model his friends had, and what they often depended on whether they lived near a Lambretta or Vespa dealer.

This meant that there tended to be more Lambrettas than Vespas around since

there were fewer Vespa dealers. But there were two other reasons why the GS had an aura of exclusivity about it. Firstly, it was impossible to make a lesser Vespa look like a GS. This was not the case with Lambrettas, and for every genuine GT200 there were several alleged GT200s of dubious origins. More about this later.

Secondly, Vespa were manufactured in Britain under license by Douglas. However, they only built the Sportique model at Bristol and imported the GS from Italy. From the point of view of Douglas it was important to sell as many Sportiques as possible in order to keep their factory busy. Consequently practically all of Douglas' contemporary advertising featured the Sportique and

not the GS.

The Sportique was a fine commuter machine with a low revving ultra reliable engine and small eight inch wheels for manourverability in traffic. These qualities did not impress mods who were more interested in power and styling. Undeterred, Douglas introduced a range of Sportique 'special editions' featuring chrome panels, metallic paint etc. A reasonable- though not huge- amount of these were sold to mods instead of a GS, most of whom suffered derision at the hands of their peers and probably regretted their choice.

The Lambretta importers had no such problems since they had no factory to keep busy. This meant that they had no inhibitions about promoting the TV/GT, a task they set about with some style.

'cool' and 'uncool' accessories and added a few of their own to create subtly (or sometimes not so subtly) different looks. In the 'cool' category were crashbars, small flyscreens, wheel discs, whitewall tyres, front bumpers , leopardskin seat covers, and chromed front and rear racks. Amongst the uncool items were flags and pennants, panniers, chrome portholes, large screens (possibly the most uncool of all) and painted racks. Over a period of time a number of 'mod' looks for scooters evolved which were subtly (or sometimes not so subtly) different from the average scooter with accessories. Generally speaking there were two main looks which lasted the duration of the mod era.

The first was the chromed look. This started off with the side panels, and

NO MATTER WHO DRIVES WHAT...

PG 228

WE ALL DRIVE **DAGENITE**LY!

Whoever you are, whatever make or model
of motor-bike or scooter you drive, you'll find
your Dagenite battery does a superb job.
It's tough, it's guaranteed, it's reliable and it's
economical. Rolls-Royce choose Dagenite —
can you do better?

DAGENITE MOTOR-CYCLE & SCOOTER BATTERIES

gradually extended to practically every part of the scooter which could be detached such as the mudguard, flywheel cover, cylinder cowling etc. Lambrettas, with their bolt-together construction, offered particular potential for this treatment, and their headset tops, horncastings and even legshields could be chromed. Mods didn't like to hang about for weeks for things to come back from the platers, so dealers soon got into the habit of supplying them on an exchange basis.

All of this could be rather expensive, especially if the main body of the scooter was resprayed as well. This was often considered desirable since chrome looked most effective against dark colours and most Vespas and Lambrettas were made in white.

Despite its expense, most of the chroming was of a dismal quality. But even if he'd known the average mod wouldn't have cared that the chrome faded after a year or so. Mod was all about living for today.

The second, and possibly most popular look was the two- toned one. Its popularity was due to a dramatic difference being created for a small financial outlay-it was even possible to do-it yourself with a few aerosol cans.

The 'spotlights and mirrors' craze erupted over the winter of 1963/64 and reached a peak during the following summer. Since most contemporary photographs of mod scooters were taken during Easter 1964, It is this image that has come to symbolise the whole if mod-even though it was an outmoded one by the end of 1964.

There were several other, lesser trends which should be noted. Firstly there was the 'skeleton' look which emerged at the end of 1964 possibly as a reaction against the excess of lights and mirrors earlier in the year. This involved removing as much of the bodywork as possible, and was a trend limited to Lambrettas because Vespas had non-detachable bodywork. There was a periodic trend to run GSs and SSs without side panels. This allowed the side-mounted spare wheel to be exposed and embellished with a white wall and a wheel disc. Unfortunately this left the electrics rather exposed, and after a few breakdowns caused by a wet ignition coil the panels normally went back on. Another style was what could be termed the 'street racer' look and which had a small following from about 1963 onwards. This involved usually a single

colour, with twin narrow stripes (fashioned from electrical insulation tape) running vertically down one side of the legshields-and sometimes on the panels too. Competition numbers could be applied either directly to the paint or on a white roundel. After it was discovered that this was illegal in the UK (and no-body wanted to give the police another excuse to stop them) the roundels were applied without the numbers. Other parts of this style were a chromed mesh guard over the headlight and spotlights mounted directly onto the legshields with chequered plastic covers over them.

Copper plating was occasionally seen as an alternative to chrome, and a late trend was to have part of the your chromed panels and mudguard painted over with a second colour- a sort of merging if the two-tone and chromed styles.

By 1966 a definitive mod scooter style had evolved which was an amalgam of all the preceding styles excepting the skeleton look . The scooter would have two tone paint and chromed engine cowlings. There would be just a couple of spot lights mounted either on crashbars or directly onto the legshields. Essential extras were a headlight grill, flyscreen, a pair of headset mounted mirrors, a sports silencer, forida style crashbars and sometimes a rear rack. If the scooter was a Vespa then 'jag' lights could be added to the list.

It was not even necessary to get all this done yourself-you could get a ready customised scooter from a dealer if you had the money. Some of the best known dealers gave their creations names. There was the Grimstead 'Hurricane'

WIN A *Vespa*

* Watch for Cliff Richard in his latest film 'Wonderful Life'

* Listen in to the David Jacobs Show on Radio Luxembourg at 10.15 on Saturday night from June 13th and hear all about Vespa.

and 50 Pakamac Bri-Nylon Scooter Coats for the runners-up in the first of three terrific " Wonderful Life " Competitions.

Full details and entry forms will be available in your local Vespa dealer's from June 10th—or in "ABC Film Review," on sale at your local ABC cinema.

IT'S HERE
THE NEW *Vespa* 90

Latest exciting addition to the Vespa range is the new 90 c.c. model. Superb design matches technical excellence at only 109½ gns. —and NO delivery charge.

Please send me full details of Vespa Scooters.

NAME_____

ADDRESS_____

Age if under 21 _____ ST.3

DOUGLAS (SALES & SERVICE) LTD., KINGSWOOD, BRISTOL. *Division of the Westinghouse Brake & Signal Co. Ltd.*

Published by the Proprietors, LINK HOUSE PUBLICATIONS LTD., 10-12 South Crescent, Store Street, London, W.C.1, and printed by Arthurs Press Ltd., Woodchester, Stroud, Glos. Agents for Australasia, Gordon & Gotch. Agents for South Africa. The Central News Agency Ltd. Printed in England.

A suspicious John Lennon look alike pictured propositioning a young female scooter rider, or is it all in our imagination?

(Vespa) and 'Imperial' (Lambretta), the Woodford 'Z Type', and the Motobaldet 'Mona' amongst others. However just about any dealer would offer you a package which included paintwork, chrome, accessories and increased power. The latter initially consisted of simply a larger barrel and piston, but by 1966 could include (unreliable) fuel injection as well. Some Dealer Vespas were given '100 mph' speedos to consolidate their new status. In some cases only the speedo face was changed-not the mechanism itself-and thus was born the legend of the '80 mph SS200'. By 1967 scooter sales were slipping drastically, and Dealer Specials became more and more outrageous in their attempts to outdo each other and grab an increased share of a declining market. For some reason the most outlandish creations were reserved for the Vespa SS 180. Motobaldet offered them with dummy petrol tanks between the legshields and seat, while Supreme Motors offered an amazing twin headlight version. The low point was surely the introduction of the Grimstead 'psychedelic' SS which was covered in flower power stickers. No better

indication was needed that the best days of mod were over.

THE SCOOTER & THE IMPECUNIOUS MOD

All the above refers to new scooters, but of course not everyone could afford such a luxury and the army of mods that regularly descended on seaside resorts always included a large number of riders of older scooters amongst their numbers. There were several different approaches which could be taken when choosing a second-hand scooter-all of them having more to do with looking flash on a budget than common sense. But then again which was more important to you when you were sixteen?

One way to get instant style was to get a GS150. In its own way it looked as good as later a GS160, and could be made to look especially good when sprayed a dark colour and fitted with chrome panels, mudguard and jag lights. Introduced in late 1954, the GS150 was light years ahead of the opposition in terms of styling and performance. Unfortunately this performance was gained at price - a high revving engine which rather tested the limits of the

Oi, Joe 90!

bearing materials and oils the available. This tended to lead to problems later in the machines life, gentle handling and regular maintenance being needed to keep some semblance of reliability. Mods were not very interested in gentle handling nor regular maintenance.

Many preferred the safer option of an LI series one or two or, even better, a TV series two -people soon learnt to avoid the catastrophically unreliable TV series one. While these models were a bit lacking in the style department, Lambretta's construction method allowed one to be updated on a gradual basis to make it look a bit more modern. The procedure for 'improving' a series one or two that had been lovingly preserved by its original owner was as follows:

The first things to go were the single seats (if fitted) to be replaced by a dual one. A cheap pattern seat caused less financial distress than a new Lambretta original, or potentially cheaper still was to scrounge someone's worn out seat and fit an imitation leopardskin cover. Next to go was the rather bulbous front mudguard , to be replaced with a slim polished alloy effort. If a series one was involved, a series two conversion was effected using a headset and horncasting obtained from a breakers. The side panels were discarded, making the scooter look more like a series three from the side.

As time went on , the increased availability of series three parts allowed for further updating into a sort of unofficial 'series two and a half'. The complete front bodywork from a series three could be fitted, together with the rear footboards. If an LI mudguard and horncasting was fitted, then these could be exchanged for GT or SX items later. The series two headset could be effectively disguised with a flyscreen . I even managed to fit a complete series three headset to a series one by filing another pinch bolt groove in the fork stem. Due to a miscalculation on my part the headset ended up ten degrees out of true, no doubt contributing to fourteen accidents in less than two years.

By 1966 it was possible to buy an early series three LI quite cheaply, at this point it became possible to create a very convincing GT or SX replica by changing the side panels, forks and headset.

It might reasonably be asked where this seemingly endless supply of nearly new spares at bargain prices was coming from. It is true that breaker's yards had plenty of insurance write-offs in them. A disproportionate number of these were GS s - Vespa monocoques not taking kindly to being crashed at speed. On the other hand, it is hard to see what kind of Lambretta write off could donate undented legshields and mudguard. The answer has to be to do with theft. Scooter theft was a big problem , and accessory theft was even more rife-things like expensive chromed side panels and floormats being almost impossible to secure.

THE MOD SCOOTER POST 1966

In December 1966 every last remaining mod tuned into the last transmission of Ready,Steady, Go!,wept a tear as Mick Jagger and Chris Farlowe joined together in a rendition of 'Out of Time' , and as the final credit ('Ready Steady Gone!) appeared either metamorphosed into hippies or entered cultural oblivion until

rescued by Sting and Phil Daniels in 1979.

Well of course they didn't, but none-the-less the public perception of mod is that there was no activity at all between 1967 and 1978. Of course it is true that there was a sharp decline, especially in London. But 'decline' doesn't equal 'nothing', and London isn't everywhere. In the London suburbs there were still plenty of mod scooters around in '67, and they still made trips to the coast in summer. There were still a reasonable number on the roads in '68, and the late following year there was a minor revival in interest as a result of the skinhead scene. However, that was just about it for the mod scooter in London for another ten years.

However, the further you went away from London the longer it took for mod scooters to disappear, and in the north they never disappeared. But that is a different story.

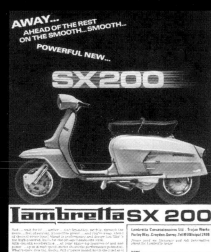

AWAY...
AHEAD OF THE REST
ON THE SMOOTH...SMOOTH...
POWERFUL NEW...

SX 200

lambretta SX 200

"Whiiill"

SANDIE SHAW

Her name may have been a bit tongue in cheek but there can be no denying her talent she came from Dagenham, Essex.. - she didn't wear shoes and she sang Puppet On a String, on The European Song Contest, she didn't win and she had great hair people have been remembered for a lot less. But I digress. Born Sandra Goodrich in Dagenham, Essex on February 26th 1947. In 1964, at the age of 17, went backstage at an Adam Faith concert, and sang for him. Faith was impressed by her voice and was immediately signed by Pye Records. Her first record "As Long As You're Happy, Baby" never charted, the but follow-up single "There's Always Something There To Remind Me" reached No. 1 in October 1964. With her trademark 'barefoot' TV and concert appearances, she epitomised the fashion of the 1960's, where she regularly appeared sporting the latest dress and knee-length white boots. In 1967 she won the Eurovision Song Contest with "Puppet On A String" (despite the success it gave her, relaunching her career which was now flagging at this point, she now refuses blankly to perform or talk about the song). BBC Television gave her her own series entitled "The Sandie Shaw Supplement" in 1968. Her last great 60's hit was Monsieur Depont in February 1969 when it reached no. 6. She retired from the pop-music world for fourteen years, until 1984 when Morrissey from The Smiths coaxed her out of retirement to record "Hand In Glove". Giving a most wonderful rendition of the song on "Top Of The Pops" when she appeared writhing on the floor of the studio. Incidentally, she has her curtains made in Blackheath!!

Recommended Listening:
"There's Always Something There To Remind Me" (1964 Pye 7N15704) "Girl Don't Come" (1964 Pye 7N 15743) "I'll Stop At Nothing" (1965 Pye 7N 15783) "Long Live Love" (1965 Pye 7N 15841) "Message Understood" (1965 Pye 7N 15940) "Tomorrow" (1966 Pye 7N 17036) "Puppet On A String" (1967 Pye 7N 17272) "Monsieur Dupont" (1969 Pye 7N 17615)

Sandie, having a measure up

JEAN SHRIMPTON

During the 1960's, Jean was the girl with the 'International Face' and soon became of the world's leading models. Dubbed "The Most Beautiful Girl In The World" many times during his period, she announced to close friends that she often got bored with being photgraphed. Born Jean Shrimpton on November 16th 1942 in Burnham, Buckinghamshire she grew up on her parents farm, and attended 'St. Bernards Convent" at Langley Road in Slough before going on to fame and fortune where she was nicknamed "The Shrimp". Along with Twiggy, she became one of the most sought after models from the period, (earning an amazing £20 an hour) frequently appearing with Mary Quant, and gracing the pages of Vogue and Elle. During 1966 she appeared hatless, gloveless, stockingless and sported a mini-skirt at the Flemington Park racecourse in Australia on 'Melbourne Cup' day. This was regarded by many as a crime on such an important day in the racing calendar, so much in fact that she was invited on to the television that night to explain her actions. "Surely people are more important than clothes?" was her reply to the media. Although she appeared regularly in the fashion media, she still remained a very private person, never regarding herself as part of the 'swinging sixties' scene. For three years she was romantically linked with another 60's 'icon' Terence Stamp, but nothing developed. In 1967 she made her big screen debut in the film "Privilege" alongside former Manfred Mann singer Paul Jones. Today, she still lives a very private life, where she was last seen running a hotel in Penzance, Cornwall. Incidently Jean's sister Chrissie was also a very familiar figure through the sixties, dating Mick Jagger and Steve Marriott.

A fine collection of Mod savouries

SMALL FACES

Dubbed by many modern-day 'pop contemporaries', such as Paul Weller and Noel Gallagher as "the most perfect pop-group" produced in Britain, the Small Faces today in the 90's are currently enjoying enormous success with a brand new legion of young fans.

Formed in May 1965, the first line-up comprised a membership of child actors Steve Marriott and James Winston, alongside Ronnie Lane and Kenny Jones. In June 1965, they were signed by Don Arden to his 'Contemporary Records' organisation, and within four months their meteoric rise to fame was complete, when their single "Whatcha Gonna Do About It" reached number 14 in the #British charts. This was followed by further chart success when in 1966, (whereas, by now Ian "Mac" McLagan had replaced Winstone on organ) "Sha-La-La-La-Lee" reached No. 3, "Hey Girl" reached No. 10 and in August of that year, "All Or Nothing" gave them their only No.1 hit. The group even moved with the 'psychedelic' times to chart with "Itchycoo Park" in August 1967.

But all was not well with the band, and at the end of the "New Years Eve" concert at the Alexandra Palace on December 31st 1968, Steve Marriott stormed off stage insisting "I am leaving the band". But due to a contracted short tour of Europe in early 1969, the final concert the group gave was not until Saturday March 8th when they bowed out at the Springfield Theatre, In Jersey, in the Channel Islands.

Marriott went on to join his friend Peter Frampton in Humble Pie, whilst Lane, McLagan, Jones and former Jeff Beck Band members Ronnie Wood and Rod Stewart would join up to form The Faces. In 1976, the best remembered line-up of Marriott, Lane, McLagan and Jones reunited briefly as the Small Faces for the re-issuing of firstly "Itchycoo Park" and then "Lazy Sunday". Both re-charted, reaching numbers 9 and 39 respectively. The reunion did not last long 'though, when during one of their first photo sessions Ronnie popped out for a packet of fags, and never returned leaving Rick Wills to cover on bass.

For the most comprehensive history of the group ever published, read "Quite Naturally : the Small Faces - A Day-By-Day guide to the career of a pop-group" - its a right riviting read!

The Small Faces hit singles 1965-1969:
"Whatch Gonna Do About It?" (Decca F 12208) September 1965
"Sha-La-La-La-Lee" (Decca F 12317) February 1966
"Hey Girl" (Decca F 12393) May 1966
"All Or Nothing" (Decca F 12470) August 1966
"My Mind's Eye" (Decca F 12500) November 1966
"I Can't Make It" (Decca F 12565) March 1967
"Here Comes The Nice" (Immediate IM 050) June 1967
"Itchycoo Park" (Immediate IM 057) August 1967
"Tin Soldier" (Immediate IM 062) December 1967
"Lazy Sunday" (Immediate IM 064) April 1968
"The Universal" (Immediate IM 069) July 1968
"Afterglow Of Your Love" (Immediate IM 077) March 1969

There'll be one along in a minute

Kenney

Plonk

Steve

and Mac

DUSTY SPRINGLFIELD

Possibly the UKs finest white female soul singer she had a string of major hits from 1964 - 1969. She went to America and recorded in Memphis for Atlantic Records the classic album, "Dusty in Memphis" and had her arse pinched live on Ready Steady Go.

THE SMOKE

Formerly known as the Shots, they were discovered playing in Yorkshire by Northern millionaire Alan Bush, whilst supporting P J Proby. The shots had released one single on the Columbia label in 1965," Keep a hold of what you've got" c/w "She's a liar" but this had failed to impress the record buying public. A name change to "The Smoke" which was the cheerful northern terminology for London, or maybe because the group smoked a lot of fags, saw the band remain with Columbia and release there only hit "My Friend Jack (eats sugarlumps)" (a cheeky reference to the Sixties habit of putting drops of liquid LSD on sugarlumps and crunching away merrily) c/w "We Can Take It". TV radio, and press followed and the Band

embarked on a successful tour of the UK and Germany (Where they released the album "Its Smoke Time". Their future looked assured until they hit upon the idea of releasing a follow up to "Jack" "I'm Only Dreaming" under the pseudonym "Chords Five". The band also underwent a complete image change from sharp Mod to far out psychedelia in a successful bid to entirely alienate their following, this resulted in confusing what audience they had left to the point that the group totally scuttled any further plans.

Classic Smoke line-up:
Mick Rowley (Vocals) Malcolm Lurker (Guitar)
John " Zeke" Lund (Bass) Geoffrey Gill (Drums)
Recommended listening:
"My Friend Jack" "It could be wonderful" (COLUMBIA).

The Smoke demonstrate their version of in-car smoke extraction and ventilation - they eventually cut down to four packs a day

TERENCE STAMP

Born in 1940, Stamp is instantly recognised as the unsmiling leading man of many a mid-sixties classic. His first film was "Term of Trial" in 1962, but it was his 1965 film "The Collector" that awarded Stamp star status, playing the part of a strange disturbed young man, who decides to add to his collection of butterflies, a beautiful young art student, played by Samantha Eggar.

In 1966, he turned down the role as the womanising-Cockney "Alfie", thus giving Michael Caine his perfect cinematic vehicle. In 1967 he appeared in "Modesty Blaise" alongside Monica Vitti, and starred in both "Far From The Madding Crowd" (alongside Julie Christie, Peter Finch and Alan Bates) and "Poor Cow", with Carol White. Later in 1969, he again let Michael Caine (who was currently broke, and sleeping on Stamp's floor) step into his shoes in a major British blockbuster, after Stamp turned down the role as Charlie in "The Italian Job". Instead he took a role in "The Mind Of Mr. Soames", playing a man who had been in a coma since birth, co-starring

with Robert Vaughn and Nigel Davenport. He remains today one of the world's most eligible bachelors.

> **Trivia note:**
> Terence Stamp was the subject of Ray Davis' classic Kinks track "Waterloo Sunset" (Terry and Julie etc, the Julie in question being Julie Christie)

SPENCER DAVIES GROUP

Spencer Davis (born on July 17th 1942 in Swansea, Wales), a former Birmingham University student, teacher and part-time blues musician Pete York (born on August 15th 1942 in Redcar, Cleveland) and the Winwood brothers Steve (born on May 12th 1948, in Birmingham) and Muff, so named after the BBC Television character 'Muffin The Mule' (born Mervyn Winwood on June

13th 1943 also in Birmingham) met at the 'Golden Eagle' pub in Birmingham. The quartet started life as 'The Rhythm & Blues Quartet' and were spotted by Chris Blackwell of Island Records on June 1st 1964. Unable to fully support his acts, Blackwell would license the group's recording output to the 'Philips' records label 'Fontana'. Their first release is the John Lee Hooker track "Dimples", but it sank without trace.

In November of 1964, their second single release, "I Can't Stand It" reaches no. 47 in the British charts and in 1965, a cover of Brenda Holloway's "Every Little Bit Hurts" reached no. 41, June saw "Strong Love" make no. 44 and on August 8th of that year, the group play on the final day of the fifth annual 'National Jazz & Blues Festival' held at the Richmond Athletic Ground in London. On September 24th, they begin a 24 date UK tour with The Rolling Stones and Unit 4 & 2 amongst others. The Stones took quite a shine to Spencer Davis, even going as so far to loan them their limousine and driver Tom Keylock while they were on an American tour. In January of 1966, their breakthrough hit came when "Keep On Running" reached no. 1, displacing The Beatles double A-side "We Can Work It Out/Day Tripper". They followed this with

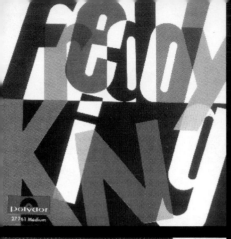

Freddy King

Polydor
27761 Medium

MAKING TIME — vogue — BIFF BANG POW
TRY AND STOP ME
SYLVETTE

THE CREATION

fontana

The Pretty Things

DON'T BRING ME DOWN
BIG BOSS MAN
ROSALYN
WE'LL BE TOGETHER

Columbia

apples and oranges

paint box

THE PINK FLOYD

THE **yaRDBIRDs**
happenings ten years time ago
psycho daisies

THE V.I.P.S I WANNA
BE FREE
DON'T LET IT GO
SMOKESTACK
LIGHTNING

fontana

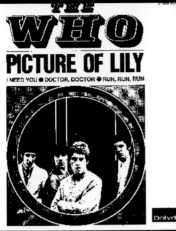

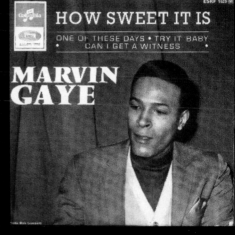

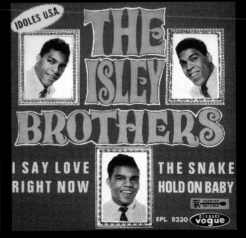

"Somebody Help Me", another no.1 in April of that year, just as they open a UK tour with The Who at the 'Gaumont Theatre' in Southampton, Hants. The group's first two albums "Their First LP" (originally released in July 1965) and "Second Album" are released in February of that year, reaching numbers 6 and 3 respectively. On May 1st, the group take part, alongside The Beatles, Rolling Stones, The Yardbirds, Small Faces and The Who, at the annual 'NME Poll Winners' concert at the Empire Pool in Wembley. On July 11th, the group enters the world of 'Pop Movies' when they begin shooting, alongside Dave Berry, the film "The Ghost Goes Gear" on location in Windsor (near Slough) and Chiddington Castle in Kent. (The film will be released in December of 1966 as a B movie to the Raquel Welch Prehistoric nonsense that was "One Million Years BC".)

In November of that year, their next big hit "Gimme Some Loving", is kept off the no.1 spot by The Beach-Boys 'masterpiece' "Good Vibrations". December 5th, the group embark on a German tour with Dave Dee & Co. In January of 1967, as 'Monkee-Madness' sweeps the World, The Spencer Davis Group release "I'm A Man" which

reaches no.9. (The song was originally written for a soundtrack on swinging London, being made by an American film company.) On March 11th, they start a 21 date UK tour with The Hollies, The Tremeloes and Paul Jones, amongst others. On March 30th they are honoured to be presented the 'Carl Alan Award' for "The Most Outstanding Group Of 1966". But shortly after, on April 2nd, both Winwood brothers would leave the band. Muff to become a record producer, and Steve to form Traffic. They were replaced by Eddie Hardin (born Edward Harding on February 19th 1949) and Phil Sawyer (born on March 8th 1947). The line-up make their debut at the annual 'NME Poll Winners Concert' at the Wembley Arena. In November, the group make an appearance during a dance sequence in the Barry Evans sex-comedy "Here We Go Round The Mulberry Bush" (which ironically featured the title track sung by ex-Spencer Davis member Steve Winwood in his new four piece band Traffic). The group also write six songs which appear on the film soundtrack and album. In August 1968, Hardin and York both depart from the group. In November of that year, with the additional line-up Dee Murray (on bass) and Dave Hynes (on drums) begin a North American tour. (Hynes will shortly be replaced by Nigel Olsson.) But in July of 1969, Davis sensibly decides enough is enough, and breaks up the Group.

Murray and Olsson go on to join Elton John, while Davis moves to California to work as a soloist.

Steve Winwood meanwhile, would enjoy three top ten hits with Traffic, namely "Paper Sun" (Island WIP 6002 - June 1967), "Hole In My Shoe" (Island WIP 6017 - September 1967), and "Here We Go Round The Mulberry Bush" (Island WIP 6025 - November 1967). A fourth single "No Face, No Name, No Number" (Island WIP 603 - March 1968) only reached no. 40. Steve, in the late 80's, re-emerged to have a big hit with "Higher Love".

Classic Spencer Davis line-up:
Spencer Davis (Vocals, Guitar) Muff Winwood (Bass) Stevie Winwood (Lead Vocals, Guitar, Hammond) Peter York (Drums)
Recommended listening:
"Somebody Help Me" Fontana TF 679
"Keep on Running" Fontana TF 632
"I'm a Man" Fontana TF 785
"Gimme Some Loving" Fontana TF 762
"Every Little Bit Hurts" (EP) Fontana TE 17450
"Here We Go Round the Mulberry Bush" (LP soundtrack with Traffic) UA SULP 1186

Left: Stevie Winwood with his famous scarf that had feet on the end.

ROD "THE MOD" STEWART

Rod was born in Scotland as Roderick David Stewart on January 10th 1945. He was taken to London at an early age by his family where he grew up. During the period 1961 to 1968 Stewart served his musical apprenticeship in various groups such as The Hoochie Coochie Men, Shotgun Express and Steam Packet alongside Brian Auger and Julie Driscol. He was highly regarded by the music industry and would regularly feature on various session work. In 1968, Stewart received his biggest break when he joined the Jeff Beck Group as the lead singer. During May and June of that year, the group toured America for six weeks. The tour was a sensation. During the concerts at the Filmore East in New York, Filmore West in San Francisco, the Grande Ballroom in Dearborn, Michigan and the Los Angeles' Shrine Auditorium, Rod received a standing ovation and the

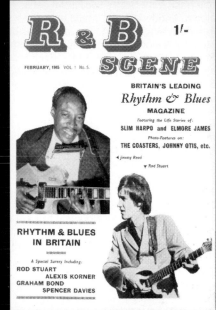

title track from Beck's successful debut album, entitled "Truth" made the American singles chart. The executives of Mercury Records were so impressed with Rod's vocals that in 1969 they signed him as a solo artist. In June of that year, Stewart joined Ian McLagan, Ronnie Lane and Kenny Jones, of the Small Faces, and former member of The Birds, Ronnie Wood. They shortened their name to the Faces and signed immediately to Warner Brothers. The group made their concert debut at Cambridge University as Quiet Melon, abley supplemented by Ronnie's elder brother Art, and another ex-Bird Kim Gardner. The Faces would go on to have many hits in the early seventies, such as "Stay With Me" (1971), "Cindy Incidentally" (1973) and "Pool Hall Richard" (1973). While Rod's solo efforts, which continue to this day, include: "Maggie May" (1971), "You Wear It Well" (1972), "Oh No, Not My Baby" (1973), "Sailing" and "This Old Heart Of Mine" (both in 1975).

Londoner born of Swedish Greek extraction released his first 45, "I Love My Dog" in 1966 for Decca Record's new avant garde label Deram. It was the beginning of an extraordinary string of successful million sellers for the singer until he suffered serious ill health problems in 1969 and disappeared from public view. He would re-emerge a year later as the sequel Cat Stevens MkII and embark on an equally successful run of albums and singles throughout the 70's. He then found the muslim faith and fancying another name change avoided the obvious MkIII suggestions and opted for the less star like Yusuf Islam. He denounced his musical roots, grew a really long beard and refused his royalties. But hey, who are we to mock, look what happened to Salman Rushdie!

Recommended Listening:
"I'm Gonna Get Me A Gun" DERAM DM 118
"Mathew & Son" DERAM DM 110
"I Love My Dog" DERAM DM 102
"Bad Night" DERAM DM 140

CAT STEVENS

Many years before Mr Yusuf Islam began his teaching career in 1979 as a North London primary school headmaster, he was known to millions as Mr Cat Stevens, recording star. Stevens, a young

UNA STUBBS

First appeared on tv in the 'rock n roll' programme "Cool For Cats" in the late 50's, but Una will always be best remembered as the long-suffering daughter of Alf Garnett in the BBCTV comedy programme "'Till Death Us Do

Below: Cat, he loved his dog

Part". Throughout the series (originally transmitted on BBC1 from June 1966) she appeared with 'Mary Quant' hairstyles, and adorned the very latest clothes that were purchased from Carnaby Street that very week the programme was recorded! She mirrored the feelings of the 'young female' and for many, was the spokesman (or rather spokewoman) for the young adult in a very changing turbulent time. Her arguments with the bigotted Garnett were a joy to behold. It is also amazing to discover, considering her young female portrayal, that when "Till Death'..." started, Una was already 29 years old! Una was born in London on May 1st 1937, and underwent training as a dancer at the 'La Roche Dancing School' in Slough, Buckinghamshire, where she resided through the sixties. Through her dancing ability, she was a perfect choice to appear in the 1963 Cliff Richard musical film "Summer Holiday". She teamed up again with Cliff & The Shadows for the film "Wonderful Life" in the following year, where she played the part of Barbara. Una naturally appeared in the 1968 big-screen version of "Till Death...", and regularly appeared with Cliff Richard in his BBCTV series, such as "The Cliff Richard Show" and "It's Cliff!".

Una married actors Peter Gilmore and then Nicky Henson in the sixties, (not at the same time) but unfortiunately, both ended in divorce. In more recent years, she gained a new legion of fans as Aunt Sally in the Southern ITV series "Worzel

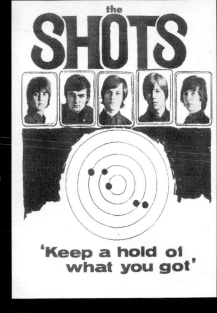

'Keep a hold of what you got'

Gummidge". She has three sons, namely Jason, Christian and Joe.

SUE RECORDS

The invention of Chris Blackwell and Guy Stevens Mod DJ from the Scene Club. Stevens saw the need for an RnB record label. A subsidiary of Island, this is the Mod label. Artists included James Brown, Ike and Tina Turner, Jimmy McGriff, Charlie and Inez Foxx. Very hard to find in mint condition with usually writing on the label/sleeve. the Mods musical taste was far superior at the time – Sue records made these sounds accessible.

Early in-band flare up - Pete accuses Roger of nicking his coat while keith can't quite remember why he's wearing two

THANK YOUR LUCKY STARS

(ABC TV Television/ ITV Network)
Produced between September 9th 1961 and June 12th 1966

Celebrated with marketing spin-offs such as hardback Christmas annuals and 'Hits of the time' compilation albums, "Thank Your Lucky Stars" was undoubtably the pop TV show of the early 1960's.

The first episode (as indeed much of the series, with recordings taking place at it's Alpha Television studios in Birmingham on a Sunday and transmitted the following Saturday 'tea-time') was hosted by Keith Fordyce and featured performances from Shani Wells and Eden Kane, alongside comedian Harry Fowler and all-rounder Kenny Lynch. (Fowler and Lynch later formed their own TV double-act).

Regular features during it's almost five years run, included 'The Confederates', a panel of teenagers and DJ's who commented on the weeks latest single releases from England and America. While the BBC's equivalent to TYLS - "Juke Box Jury"- reviewed new singles as either 'Hits' or 'Misses', the TYLS panel marked the songs out of ten. This spawned the national catchphrase, "Oi'll give it foive", uttered from the mouth of Birmingham babe Janice Nichols. Such was the extent of Janice's 'fifteen minutes of fame', Decca Records, in February 1963, signed her up for a one-

off single entitled "I'll Give It Five". "Thank Your Lucky Stars" had an obvious advantage over the BBC's 'Juke Box Jury' in that, instead of the records merely being played, TYLS featured the likes of The Beatles, The Rolling Stones and The Kinks, amongst others, actually appearing personally to lip-synch their latest release.

During it's five year run, the format for the show remained the same. (a major factor in it's eventual cancellation). The exceptions being a change of host, when 'Carry-on' stalwart Jim Dale was introduced around Easter of 1966, the introduction of a dance group, featuring choreography by Jo Cook (fresh from the BBC2 pop show 'The Beat Room', whose previous dance troupe 'The Go-Jos', laid the groundwork to the legendary 'Top Of The Pops' outfit 'Pan's People') and the change of broadcast day, when, also in 1966, it moved to a Sunday afternoon slot. Besides classic performances from the fore-mentioned Beatles and Stones, the producers also went to great lengths to specially import from the States, The Lovin' Spoonful to appear on the show transmitted April 24th 1966.

There's no chance, unfortunately, of a "Best Of Thank Your Lucky Stars" companion series, as only one complete episode remains in the ABCTV archives. (This one derives from May 15th 1966, and features The Rolling Stones, alongside Tom Jones and The Koobas, performing "Lady Jane" and "Paint It Black"). While loads of other clips ('inserts') featuring The Beatles, Cilla, The Searchers and Gerry & The Pacemakers, amongst others, still

The mad old badger Van the man Morrison with Them

feel a song title coming on... how about "Jimmy"

survive, but have yet to be returned to the archives. Janice Nichols, meanwhile, gave up the heady world of TV stardom to become a foot beautician!!

TWIGGY

Born in Kilburn, London in 1949 as Lesley Hornby, Twiggy, in the 1960's, with her waife-like 32-22-32 figure, was one of the country's top models. She had no bust, carried a male haircut and looked extremely frail. She was in complete contrast to the 'hourglass' figures epitomised by 1950's women. At her peak in the mid 60's, she was earning up to £80 an hour for modelling jobs in New York. (This was an absolute fortune for the day. The average British teenager was only earning about £15 a week!) She even launched a range of Twiggy fashions. Her designer dresses and suits were selling up to 15,000 items a week. You were even able to purchase Twiggy coathangers!
Her big break came at the age of 15, when she started dating the 25 year-old hairdresser Justin de Villeneuve, and it was him that arranged her first photo session. Justin also changed her name to Twiggy. (Apparently because her legs

looked like twigs!) When this relationship fizzled out, she started to date 27 year-old Nigel Davis. Even though she had immense fame and wealth, she still insisted on living with her dear Mum at 93, St. Raphael's Way in Neasden.
As the 60's drew to a close, she turned her hands to acting, where later she won rave reviews in Ken Russell's musical film "The Boyfriend", and in the part of Eliza Doolittle in "Pygmalion". In August of 1976 she had a top twenty hit with the song "Here I Go Again" (Mercury 6007 100). In 1977, she married the actor Michael Whitney. They had a daughter called Carly. Unfortunately Michael died in 1983, shortly after the couple had seperated. Twiggy went on to marry another actor, Leigh Lawson, star of 'The Travelling Man'.

TWINKLE

Twinkle was born Lyn Ripley in 1947. During her brief time at the Guildhall School Of Music, she took up classical music. But it was at the age of seventeen as Twinkle, she recorded the controversial teenage anthem "Terry". The song, which reached No. 4 in December of 1964, concerned the exploits of a teenage motorbiker who responds to a lover's tiff by roaring into the night to his death. The song caused so much of a stir at the time that "Ready Steady Go!" banned the song, emminent writer Ted Wills called the song "dangerous drivel!" and, in an attempt to travel to America with the song in 1965, she had her work permit refused. "Oh well", she sighed, "I shall have to stay at home working on my novel about the ups and downs of adolescence." But all was not lost with the single, when the "pirate" stations played it repeatedly, and in a show, which also featured The Beatles and The Rolling Stones, she performed the song at the "1965 NME Poll Winners Poll Concert" at the Empire Pool, Wembley.

Thankfully, she was also coaxed out of her home to accompany her Decca labelmates the Bachelors on a tour of Australia and New Zealand in 1965. That same year, in February, her follow-up, and only other chart success, "Golden Lights" (or rather AKA, "Terry" part 2) entered the charts. In recent years, Lyn (Twinkle) has seen the lucrative money that can be made by the "Solid Sixties" golden oldie hit tours, where she was seen again performing well…

Trivia note:
Twinkle had follow ups to Terry with such memorable titles as "Tommy", "Poor Old Johnny" and later "Micky". Alas the formula was not to work.

Recommended Listening:
"Terry" DECCA F 12013

Brian Epstein in association with Radio London presents

GEORGIE FAME | JULIE FELIX

SOUNDS INCORPORATED ❀ CAT STEVENS
THE FOURMOST ❀ THE GEORGIE FAME ORCHESTRA conducted by HARRY SOUTH

SAVILLE THEATRE FOR 2 WEEKS ONLY from BOXING DAY

SHAFTESBURY AVENUE TEMple Bar 4011 ★ AT 6.10 & 8.45 BOOK NOW 20/- to 6/-

FUNNY GIRL BOUTIQUE

Step out in flower boots

Funny Girl (Birmingham) Limited
9 The Bullring, Birmingham

Miss Snoopy
3 Barton Street, Bath

Miss Snoopy
23 Castle Street, Cardiff

Funny Girl (Norwich) Limited
2 Dove Street, Norwich

Funny Girl (Manchester) Limited
17 Old Bank Street, Manchester

Head Office
15a & 16 Milsom Street, Bath
Bath 63067/8/9

Funny Girl (Cardiff) Limited
23 Castle Street, Cardiff

Funny Girl (Bristol) Limited
11 Clare Street, Bristol

Funny Girl (Bath) Limited
1 Burton Street, Bath

Funny Girl (Edinburgh) Limited
88 Shandwick Place, Edinburgh

Funny Girl (Leeds) Limited
20 Queen Victoria Street, Leeds 1

Funny Girl (W.S.M.) Limited
19 Dolphin Square
Weston Super Mare

TOP OF THE POPS — THAT'S ... TIZER!

Happy!
Tizer
THE APPETIZER

UP THE JUNCTION

(Paramount Pictures-
September 1967)
The film, based on the
book by Neil Dunn,
starred Suzy Kendall as a
young Chelsea girl (Polly)
who decides to give up her
rich and comfortable lifestyle and seek
her own independence in Battersea.
Firstly taking a cheap job in a packing
factory where she meets Sylvie (played
by Maureen Lipman) and her sister Rube
(Adrienne Posta), and then, during her
moval into a rented 'dingy' flat, meets
Peter, played by Dennis Waterman. Their
relationship flourishes, but it all ends in
tragedy, when, following a weekend
away in Brighton in a Jag. that Peter had
stolen in order to impress her, Polly
admits that she does not want all the
luxuries that she has, whereas this is
ironically exactly what Peter is striving
for. Following an appearance in court,
Peter is sentenced to jail for stealing
the car.
The film wonderfully portrays the
seedier side of suburban London life
during the decade, where 'illegal'
abortion and irresponsible
behaviour is a part of life. The film
went on to become the "Top
Moneymaker of 1968".
(Produced by Anthony Havelock-
Allan and John Brabourne, and
directed by Peter Collinson.
Running time 119 minutes -
colour Certificate (x)).

the junction
It's rough, raw, and randy!

SUZY KENDALL · DENNIS WATERMAN

If you haunt the London clubs like the 'Scene' and the 'Flamingo', then don't be surprised if this week's Undiscovered British Boyfriend looks vaguely familiar to you. For 21-year-old Peter Meaden admits he's more often out enjoying the London night life than at home! And this isn't only because he likes the clubs—although that's true, too—but because Peter is one of the behind-the-scene boys in the pop world, and he thinks it's disastrous for anyone in the pop world to get out of touch with the trends. Actually, Peter is one of the people who set them. You've probably heard a lot about tickets and faces lately, well, Peter's a face!

Auburn-haired and blue-eyed, Peter's just a fraction under 6 ft. He was at grammar school and then he left for art school with five 'O' levels and two 'A's to his credit. Art school lasted about one year! Later, Peter had left both school and home for a flat in Hampstead and a job in an advertising agency.

After that—another agency. Then he joined up with Andrew Oldham (the Stones' manager) to form an advertising agency, until last year when he left the country for seven months. After making some money in Spain and North Africa—'something to do with cars'—Peter arrived back in England and almost immediately flew off for a vacation in America for three weeks. He gets around, this boy!

Back from the States, Peter tried his hand as a free-lance photographer and journalist for a while, then finally joined up again with his old partner Andrew Oldham, handling publicity for the Crystals, Gene Pitney and the Stones.

BOYFRIEND

UNDISCOVERED british

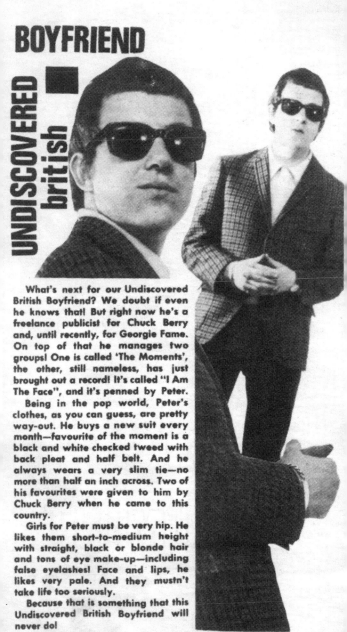

What's next for our Undiscovered British Boyfriend? We doubt if even he knows that! But right now he's a freelance publicist for Chuck Berry and, until recently, for Georgie Fame. On top of that he manages two groups! One is called 'The Moments', the other, still nameless, has just brought out a record! It's called "I Am The Face", and it's penned by Peter.

Being in the pop world, Peter's clothes, as you can guess, are pretty way-out. He buys a new suit every month—favourite of the moment is a black and white checked tweed with back pleat and half belt. And he always wears a very slim tie—no more than half an inch across. Two of his favourites were given to him by Chuck Berry when he came to this country.

Girls for Peter must be very hip. He likes them short-to-medium height with straight, black or blonde hair and tons of eye make-up—including false eyelashes! Face and lips, he likes very pale. And they mustn't take life too seriously.

Because that is something that this Undiscovered British Boyfriend will never do!

VESPAS

For everything you need to know about Vespas and some things you couldn't care less about see Scooters. A marked lack of subjects in the 'V' category meant we had to resort to showing a couple of Very rare records, so here are…

VERY RARE RECORDS

A really, really, really rare record - pre Small Faces Steve Marriott offering with his band The Moments, and an even rarer than rare test pressing of The Small Faces hit "Tin Soldier"

THE WHO - THE HIGH NUMBERS

Pete Meaden, top "face" during the early days of the original Mod movement, assured his near legendary status, when he took his own life in the mid-seventies. He's widely acknowledged as the man who got the ball rolling for the Who, after manouvering his way into position of co-manager, alongside Helmut Gordon, in 1964. It was Meaden who first introduced the Detours (as the band were then known) to the clothes-mad world of Mod and carefully planned the group's new identity and name, The High Numbers, by launching them as the country's first performing Mod band. They released one single as The High Numbers ("I'm The Face"/"Zoot Suit", on Fontana Records), to little or no interest. The group gamely gigged around for a few months under the increasingly bizarre guidance of Meaden before his pill popping habits rendered him too unreliable and unable to make decisions. He was replaced at the helm by two assistant film directors, Kit Lambert and Chris Stamp (brother of actor, Terence), on the look out for a group, as the subject of a proposed documentary. After seeing the band in action at the Railway Tavern, Harrow, the film idea was forgotten and the pair became the group's managers. By now, the band were calling themselves "The Who", a name suggested by guitarist Pete Townshend's Ealing Art College friend, Richard Barnes. (They were toying with "The Hair And The Who", until somebody pointed out it sounded like the name of a pub!). With Lambert's flair for promotion and Stamp's street suss, a visually striking white on black poster, (with Townshend mid-power chord), promising "Maximum R & B", was designed and flyposted all over London. The band made a devastating impact on Tuesday night audiences at the Marquee, with Pete Townshend's "Birdman" windmilling chords and feedback solos, Keith Moon's demented thrashing on the kit, singer Roger Daltrey screaming himself hoarse, while ,John Entwistle, anchored the mayhem down with dive-bombing bass runs. It was this Tuesday night residency that laid the foundations for the group's transition from London club obscurity to world domination.

Classic Action line up:
Pete Townshend (Guitar, vocals) Roger Daltrey (Vocals)
John Entwistle (Bass, vocals) Keith Moon (Drums, vocals)
Recommended Listening:
"My Generation" (album) BRUNSWICK LAT 8616
"Ready Steady Who" (EP) REACTION 592001

Hello... Who?

The orrible "Oo"

DAVE WEDGEBERRY

Decca Records in house photographer responsible for the classic images that adorned The Who's My Generation and The Small Faces Debut. Big give away of Dave's style and inspiration was that 90% of all his shots were taken within walking distance of Deccas embankment offices, The Who with Big Ben behind them is a case in point.

WHISKY-A-GO-GO

The Whisky-A-Go-Go was situated at 33-37 Wardour St. It opened in 1962 in the same building that once housed the famous Flamingo Club. The Go-Go, although not strictly a live music venue, was *the* London all night Mod spot. It was also the frequent watering hole of bands and artists that had just finished their sets some hundred yards along the road at the Marquee. It was a particular favourite of The Stones, The Action, David Bowie and The Who. It shortened its name in the early 80's and became "The Wag".

WOODFORD SCOOTERS

Essex scooter shop specialising in chrome and accessorised scooters famous for the Vespa SS200 Woodford Z type complete with 12 volt conversion. There are only 2 known to remain intact.

PAUL WELLER

Post 60's Mods' most celebrated "Mod Geezer" Weller probably out Mods the best of his latterday contemporaries and even a few of the originals. His band The Jam arguably rose to become the most important group in the UK during the late half of the 70's and early part of the 80's. Weller, obviously in love with all the facets of the Mod phenomenon, draws constantly on its fashions, but adds his own original accessories creating a style all of his own. Now as a solo performer he continues to turn on a new generation to all things Mod.

Advert for The Twisted Wheel, Manchester's seminal Mod Club

Weller having picked up his fags and, one assumes, supped up his beer.

JIMMY WINSTON

Jimmy Winston, the Small Faces' original keyboard player, unceremoniously sacked by the group (he turned up for a gig at tha Lyceum to find his replacement Ian McLagan already filling his shoes…charming). He was kept on at Decca Records after forming his own group, Jimmy Winston's Reflections, after he cheekily released the Marriott/Lane composition "Sorry She's Mine". this failed to chart and the Reflections became Winston's Thumbs. They released the equally doomed "Real Crazy Apartment" backed with "Snow White". Jimmy faded into obscurity, and is forever remembered as the bloke who was too tall to be a Small Face!

PETER WYNGARDE

Peter Wyngarde, better known as suave, moustached, crime-sleuth Jason King with his flared trousers in the late 60's. Born in Marseilles, France (year unknown) he started his working life in advertising before venturing into the showbiz world, where he was gainfully employed at Bristol's 'Old Vic' theatre. Peter made his New York stage debut in 1960 and made his big-screen debuts in the films 'The Innocents', 'Siege Of Sidney Street' (1960), 'Flash Gordon' and the creepy horror film, 'Night Of The Eagle' in 1962.
But it was as secret agent Jason King in 'Department S' that his fame really took off! The series (shown in England on the ITV network between March 1969 and March 1970) concerned an unusual police department which was a branch of 'Interpol'. The wide range of bizarre plots that King and his assistants were called in to solve included dead wives returning from the grave, blackmail, villages where all its inhabitants vanished, espionage and murder. Such was his popularity, he was even voted "The Best Dressed Man Of 1970".
When "Deptartment S" finished, Wyngarde, considering he was the main star of the programme, naturally returned in a follow-up ITC series called 'Jason King'. The series was not as successful as its predesessor ?? and was soon axed. All through his television carreer, he was regularly surrounded by a bevy of beautiful young (and mature) females. But in 1974, he reached a low-point in his life, when he was caught having relations with men in the public toilets. Wyngard remains today a real character, where he returned to the Theatre and recently appeared in "Doctor Who" for he BBC. Meanwhile, due to the advent of Satelitte Television, he can still be seen in his role as Jason King in the repeated re-runs.

Below: Jimmy Winston and the Reflections

Where did you park it?

Jimmy took to having huge guitars made in an attempt to make himself look smaller

Hailing from Surrey, The Yardbirds were among the most prominent of the many English R&B bands emerging from the South. However, what set them apart from the

1966, it was Beck's idea to introduce his friend, Jimmy Page, into the fold. (Page had initially been approached to replace Clapton, but declined due to his lucrative employment as a sessionman), It was this Beck-Page twin-guitar line-up (with Chris Dreja now on bass), that was captured to great effect in Michelangelo Antonioni's Mod "Swing London" film,

competition, was eighteen year old guitarist, Eric Clapton, who was able to effortlessly reproduce the sound and feel of authentic Chicago rhythm and blues. The band were managed by Giorgio Gomelsky and, thanks to this connection, took over the Rolling Stones residency at the legendary Crawdaddy Club in Richmond. Columbia Records signed them up in 1964, relaying two singles ("I Wish You Would" and "Good Morning Little Schoolgirl") and an album ("Five Live Yardbirds"), recorded live at the Marquee, that perfectly encapsulates the excitement of the era. Clapton was way the bands most Mod-conscious member with close-cropped hair, turned-up Levi's and desert boots, that inspired many emulators. Dissatisfied with the bands commercial direction, Clapton quit in 1965, to be replaced by another Surrey flamboyant whizz-kid, Jeff Beck. The band achieved their greatest success with this line-up. When bassist Paul Samwell-Smith left in

"Blow Up" (1966). Beck left shortly thereafter and the four-piece line-up soldiered on for another eighteen months, finally calling it a day in July, 1968.
Page picked up the pieces to form a new "supergroup", Led Zeppelin, but that's another story....

Classic Yardbirds line up:
Keith Relf (vocals, harmonica), Chris Dreja (guitar), Jim McCardy (drums), Paul Samwell-Smith (bass), Eric Clapton (guitar 1963-1965), Jeff Beck (guitar 1965-1966), Jimmy Page (guitar 1966-1968).
Recommended listening:
"I Wish You Would" COLUMBIA DB 7283
"Heart Full of Soul" COLUMBIA DB 7594
"Over, Under, Sideways, Down" (EP) COLUMBIA SEG8521
"Five Live Yardbirds" (LP) COLUMBIA 33SX1677

Five birds, one chick, four hits.

New! Perfumed Hair Spray. With Lanolin. Holds your hair in swinging shape, even on drizzle-damp days. Strictly no lacquer.

New! Perfumed Talc. Extra smooth texture. For all-over all-day freshness.

Miss Disc Talc

Miss Disc Cologne

Miss Disc Hair Spray

Miss Disc Spray Deodorant

New! Perfumed Cologne. Light, fresh, gorgeously stimulating. And it lasts and lasts and lasts!

New! Perfumed deodorant. Spray on in seconds and stay cool-cool fresh all around the clock.

Available from Boots and leading chemists.

She's the chick among the Yardbirds. She goes for groups. They go for her. She has her very own group too. Named after her. Miss Disc. A very 'in' group, indeed. Led by the most sensational, fab, _new_ kind of hair spray. Tames her hair when it's wild. But just enough. No more. Great. Everything under control. Yet breathtakingly alive! Miss Disc has your kind of group for your kind of person. Get together. Soon!

The latest release by the Yardbirds — "Happenings Ten Years Time Ago"

Miss Disc
Perfumed with 'Men in Mind'

quant afoot

9 BELOW ZERO

Formed on 1978 as Stan's Blues Band they started their musical life as South London's Dr Feelgood. They quickly gained a reputation as Londons hottest live draw after demolishing both the Feelgoods and the Blues Band on London Weekend's South Bank Show. Despite regular sold out English and European tours which included headlining a capacity Hammersmith Odeon supported by Alexis Korner, and an unprecedented ammount of TV coverage which included the now legendary "Young Ones" and "OTT" singles success was to sadly elude them. They called it a day on the eve of the release of what could arguably have been their breakthrough album "Third Degree".

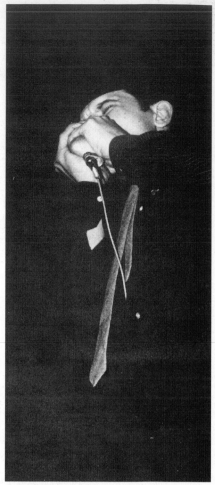

Trivia note:
"Third Degree"s album cover was photographed by David Bailey while their previous album "Don't Point Your Finger" was produced by Glyn Johns (Rolling Stones, Faces)

Classic 9 Below Zero line up:
Dennis Greaves (guitar, vocals); Mark Feltham (harmonica, vocals); Peter Clark (bass, vocals); Micky Burcky (drums).
Reccommended listening:
"Live at the Marquee" (LP) A&M 397194-2 French CD
"Don't Point Your Finger" A&M 394859-2 French CD
"Third Degree" A&M 540167-2 French CD
"Covers" ZED 001 CD

Above: Mark Feltham currently blowing a storm with Oasis.
Below: 9 Below Zero "Live at the Marquee"

During a rare lull in NBZ's set, Dennis could always be relied upon to entertain the crowd by balancing a boiled egg on his head

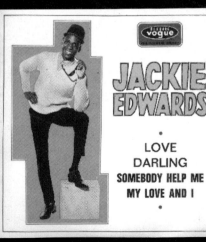

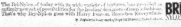

Thanks to:

Martin Costello, David Wedgbury,
Roch Vidal, Guy Joseph,
Mandi O'Connor, Art Wood,
Paul McEvoy, Julian Potter, Andy Neil,
Tony Lordan, Tony Gayle, Glen Marks,
Peter Chalcraft, John Hellier, Paul
Newman, Gary Crowley, Dennis Greaves,
Richard Barnes, John Reid,
Pictorial Press, Paul Hallam, Darren
Russell and Mark Waine.

Also special thanks to Bill "the Cab"
Riley published here for the first time.
And an extra nod to Guy Joseph.